COLLINS GEM

TRAVEL GAMES

The Diagram Group

HarperCollins*Publishers*

HarperCollins Publishers
P.O. Box, Glasgow G4 0NB

A Diagram Book first created by Diagram Visual
Information Limited of 195 Kentish Town Road,
London NW5 8SY, England

First published 1992
© Diagram Visual Information Limited 1992
Reprint 10 9 8 7 6 5 4 3 2 1 0

ISBN 0 00 470042 2

Printed in Great Britain by
HarperCollins Manufacturing, Glasgow

Introduction

Searching for amusement on a long and boring journey
can be frustrating, especially for harassed parents
travelling with restless, energetic children. *Collins
Gem Travel Games* is a helpful, exhaustive and highly
illustrated directory to a variety of imaginative games
and activities that are suitable for playing when
travelling. The games (such as spotting games, word
games, quizzes and guessing games) and activities
(such as paper folding, cat's cradle, making wool balls
and knitting on a bobbin) will occupy those with
inquiring minds as well as those who simply enjoy
playing games for their own sake. A variety of the
games included here can be swapped around regularly
or played simultaneously, to provide a greater
challenge.

For ease of reference, the games and activities have
been listed according to their suitability for certain
types of travel, whether by road, rail, sea or air.
Advice is also given on how to prepare for an amusing
journey and on what to include in a 'travel pack'.
Created by the Diagram Group, *Collins Gem Travel
Games* is an attractive companion volume to the same
team's *Gem Family and Party Games*, *Gem Card
Games* and *Gem Games for One*.

Contents

Travelling with children: handy hints

GAME SELECTION

Games should be chosen with children's abilities and temperaments in mind. Small children seldom help with the smooth running of a game for.which they have little aptitude or patience. Most children become bored with a game that does not have early results. Older children's enthusiasm soon wanes if a game is interrupted. It is best to stop games as soon as one of the players distracts the others from the intentions of the game. Vary the types of game, and do not allow any game to continue beyond the players' attention spans. Various kinds of game should be tried so that, even if one participant excels at a game or type of game, the same person does not always win.

Throughout the book, the games and activities are marked, with the symbols given below, indicating the types of travel for which they are most suitable.

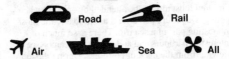

Road   Rail

Air   Sea   All

TRAVELLING BY ROAD

Car sickness needs to be avoided, so games that require reading or writing are not recommended. Observational games, such as those which involve looking at roadside activities, or quizzes are best for the confines of a moving car.

It is a good idea for the eldest child (minimum age 12) to sit in the front passenger seat, while an adult sits in the rear with the other children. Unattended children in the back seats can be a recipe for trouble.

TRAVELLING BY RAIL OR AIR

During long rail or air journeys, children will want to wander up and down the aisles. They should be escorted by an adult and should be asked to be quiet and not to annoy the other passengers.

In the confines of aeroplanes and trains, activities which require concentration and study, such as those involving drawing and writing, can hold the child's attention for long periods of time.

This type of journey affords good opportunities to write stories or letters. While travelling home, creating a diary of the daily occurrences encountered, either in writing or as a series of pictures, can prove to be a satisfying activity. These diaries may, in later years, be a pleasant way to remember the journey's events.

TRAVELLING BY SEA

Children must always be attended by an adult when sailing. Departure and arrival are probably the most interesting part of a sea trip. There is so much of interest in harbours and at docks. Time can be spent viewing from the deck or portholes. During the journey, if the sea is calm, games of concentration can be played. Almost all ships have tables at which children can sit and play pencil and paper games.

Travel pack

Select a small suitcase, shoulder bag or old briefcase in which to pack objects to be used while on the journey. If a suitcase is chosen then it can be used as a play surface when it is put on the knees of a seated player. As the travel pack will contain a variety of things, it is a good idea to use separate, small containers in which to keep various pieces of string, counters, scissors, etc. Elastic bands can be used to bind pencils and pens together, so that they are easily accessible. Organizing the travel pack in this way will prevent frustration when trying to find the objects needed for a particular game. Before setting out on a journey, make one child responsible for the travel pack and for gathering everything up after the playing session.

Put familiar objects in the travel pack, such as favourite storybooks or small toys. The following are also very useful on long journeys: cassettes of music and books (especially when travelling by car); travel board games, such as solitaire, and magnetic chess and draughts; and a pack of cards.

A variety of objects that may be useful for playing the games described in this book should also be included.

BASIC OBJECTS

Pencils and a sharpener

Do not pack a knife for sharpening pencils, as this may cause accidents. Also, pack a small plastic bag to use for gathering up the pencil sharpenings and discarded paper.

Colouring pencils
These can be great fun if a colouring book or a pad of
strong paper are packed. The travellers are then able to
draw imaginative pictures.

Ball-point and felt-tipped pens
Be careful, as these can stain hands and clothes.

Scissors
Only if travelling by aeroplane or train. It is dangerous
to take scissors on car journeys. The type of scissors to
be included should be small, with round ends, and
suitable for cutting paper.

Paper
Large quantities of cheap paper (if possible, including
graph and ruled paper) come in useful for games,
drawing or even paper folding.

Paper clips and wing clasps
These are needed for making paper toys, such as
a paper helicopter (see p. 204) and a story wheel
(see p. 138). Also, if desired, they are useful for
keeping together pieces of paper from various games.

Used matches
A large box of used matches is often useful. Matches
can be used as markers, counters and to keep track of
the number of games won. For example, the child with
the most matches at the end of a journey is the overall
winner.

A watch with a second hand
Timing the duration of a game can heighten excitement.
If travelling by car or train, a watch can also be used to
judge distance.

Play-Doh™ or Plasticine™

For smaller children this can be a source of endless fun through modelling animals, people and objects. It is essential that all the pieces are gathered up after playing because Play-Doh™ and Plasticine™ tend to stick to clothes, floors and upholstery.

A compass

For games involving the use of direction.

Lengths of string

Useful for cat's cradle and similar games. Find out which lengths are the most comfortable for the players before starting on your journey. String that is too short can be frustrating and string that is too long may be hard to control, causing the string figures to sag.

Newspapers

If these have been bought and read during a journey, they can be used subsequently for paper-folding games.

Dictionaries and an atlas

For older children, the *Collins Gem English Dictionary* and (if travelling abroad) foreign language dictionaries can be useful. A *Collins Gem Atlas of Britain* or *Gem Atlas of the World*, or a road atlas may prove useful when playing some word games that use place names.

Tubs of wet tissues or a damp cloth

Invaluable for sticky fingers and assorted accidents!

Games to play: by journey

ALL ✘

ROAD 🚗

RAIL 🚂

AIR ✈

SEA

1. Spotting games

These games, in which players try to spot as many examples of a certain object or type of object as possible, have limitless possibilities. Although most spotting games are for car journeys, many are suitable for other ways of travelling and can be easily adapted. Most can be played by as many or as few players as are available, but make sure one person – the driver or, preferably, another adult, acts as referee to resolve disagreements and to keep score if players want to play several rounds.

Once all the games in this book have been tried, players can make up their own by selecting other objects for spotting that are unique to their journey.

LOTS OF LEGS ✖

In this game players count the number of legs on objects, people and animals. For more of a challenge,

Examples for Lots of Legs

one leg   two legs   three legs

players can look for 'legs' in words, such as on signs or maps.

Playing

As a player spots a subject, he or she calls out the number of legs and points out the subject to the other players. Each player tries to find an example of as many groups of legs as possible.

The fun is in being creative with the selection. A shop sign with a mermaid would produce one leg; an old man with a walking stick would produce three legs. Legs can also be found in words on signs, and in maps and newspapers. For example, there is one 'leg' in legal, and three 'legs' can be found in the sentence 'Eleanora giggles longer'.

Winning

Players can agree beforehand on a time limit for the game, or they can agree the number of legs each player must spot.

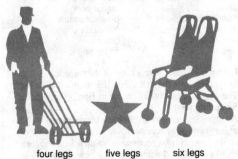

four legs   five legs   six legs

SPOT THE GARMENT 🚶 ✈ 🚢

This spotting game can be as easy or as difficult as the players choose to make it.

Playing

Before going on a train, boat or plane (it is difficult to play on a car journey), players make a list of garments and accessories they are likely to spot on people they see, such as fellow passengers.

The list could include such items as hats, gloves, shoes, ties and scarves, but they must be items of a certain type or colour. For example, on the list might be a red tie, a blue hat, a pair of white gloves, ski boots or a police officer's hat. Other items to spot might be jewellery and accessories, such as spectacles or headphones, or even different hairstyles.

Here are a few more examples:

bicycle helmet	handkerchief
'wrap-around' sunglasses	wellingtons
shawl	blazer badge
hooded parka	plastic sandals
string of pearls	Bermuda shorts
life jacket	braces
tie pin	finger rings

Each player must have a copy of the same list, and as the players spot the items they tick them off their list. The player to tick off all the items first is the winner.

Swap and spot

A surprising variation is for each player to make up his or her own list of accessories to spot. After setting off on the journey, players must swap their lists and then try to tick off all the items on their new, 'surprise' list.

Items to spot on a man

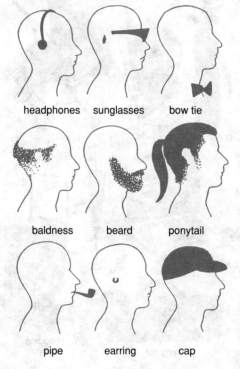

headphones sunglasses bow tie

baldness beard ponytail

pipe earring cap

golf clubs   rucksack   pram

briefcase

umbrella

carry cot

shopping
buggy

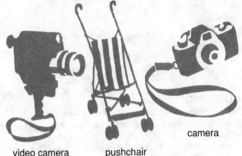

video camera   pushchair

camera

SPOT THE OBJECT ✖

In this game, players select an object from a list made
before the journey, and the winner of the game is the
first person to spot his or her choice. Players can also
choose an object for each other to spot.

The less ordinary the objects, the more difficult they are
to spot, and the more fun the game will be. But try to
select likely objects, such as a rucksack if the journey is
to the countryside, a pram or pushchair if travelling by
train, or a briefcase if you are in an airport.

Spot the object with the...

A variation of Spot the Object, this game calls for
players to select (for themselves or another player to
spot) an object of a certain type and colour. For
instance, the object chosen might be a blue umbrella, a
green rubbish bin or a purple sign. Again, the first
player to spot such an object wins.

GOT 'EM ✖

In this game players try to spot people wearing distinctive clothing or uniforms that show what kind of jobs they do.

Before setting out, make a list of people by occupation and assign points to each profession or type. The number of points will depend on how likely it is that the person will be spotted: on a train journey, a motorcycle messenger might be worth 20 points, but a ticket inspector might be worth only 5. Other occupations connected with travel include police officers, road sweeps, customs officials and flight attendants. Players need not restrict their spotting to travelling personnel; look also for soldiers, nurses and nuns.

The winner is the person who spots the most on the list by the end of the journey.

Animal got 'em

A variation of Got 'Em, this game requires players to look for animal types. The kinds of animals that are spotted will depend on the journey: in the countryside, you can spot cows, horses, pigs and sheep; in towns or cities – or even in airports – you will mostly spot dogs or birds. In that case, look for different breeds of dogs such as hounds, terriers or poodles, or for different types of birds.

Be sure to assign a value to each type of animal, not to each creature seen. Otherwise, you might be trying to count a herd of cattle while passing at high speed!

PHONEBOX FOLKS 🚗 🚤 ✈

Lots of fun can be had while waiting at airports, train
stations or motorway service stations by looking at
people in telephone booths and imagining what their
situations are. (Phones are sometimes in phoneboxes,
but more often they are set up as a 'bank' of telephone
booths.) When playing these games be careful not to
annoy the people you see; you can keep your distance
and still play a variety of telephone booth games.

Odd and evens

This game is for two players only. It requires players to
go into telephone booths, and it can only be played with
vacant booths.

Each telephone has a number, printed just below where
the handset sits. One player chooses odd and the other

even, and both look for telephone numbers that end in a number in their chosen categories. The player who collects the most wins.

Men or women

A game for two players only. One player chooses men as his or her category and the other player chooses women. Then both players try to find as many phone booths as possible with occupants in that chosen category.

Time's up

Players need a watch for this game.

Each player selects a particular telephone booth, and the winner is the one whose occupant is in the booth for the longest time.

ON THE JOB 🚗 🏎 ✈

There are always people working, and spotting them is
an easy game to play – and a fun way to pass the time –
as you wait in motorway cafes, stations, airports, or
even if you are passing through town in a car.
Before the journey, each player selects ten workers –
men and women – to make up a varied list.

Winning

As players spot a person on their list, they tick off that
person and get a point. If a player spots a person on
another player's list, the player whose list it is loses one
point. The winner is the player with the most points at
the end of the journey.
Here are some illustrated examples of working people
to put on a list:

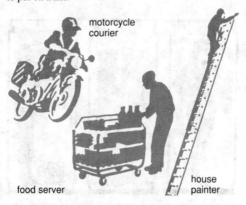

motorcycle
courier

food server

house
painter

builder

telephone engineer

bricklayer

road repairer

road sweeper

carpenter

SPOT THE SHAPE ✖

This spotting game can be played however and
wherever you travel: in the country, in towns, inside
vehicles or waiting rooms, or even in the pages of
books and magazines.

Each player must find an example of each of the basic
shapes shown on this page. Shapes can be hidden, for
example, in roofs or shapes of buildings, road signs or
on vehicles.

For a more challenging variation, each player could be
required to find examples of the shapes in different
colours – blue, green, red or yellow.

a triangle
b square
c pentagon (five-sided)
d hexagon (six-sided)
e heptagon (seven-sided)
f octagon (eight-sided)

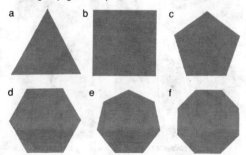

SPOT THE BUILDING 🚗 🚄

While travelling by train or car you may pass buildings
that are typical of particular regions you travel through:
an oast house in the southeast English countryside, for
example, or a tower block in the city. As players spot a
building type, they call it out; that type cannot be called
out again even if spotted later. The player who called it
out gets one point. If a player calls out a building
already spotted he or she loses a point.

Winning

Players agree a time limit beforehand. The player with
the most points at the end of the game wins.

On the next two pages are illustrations of buildings and
structures you may encounter on your journey. Use
them as a guide to help identify types.

1 tall block of flats
2 factory with chimneys
3 cathedral or large church
4 statue of a local dignitary
5 storage tank in a gas works
6 castle
7 oast house (only found in southeast England)
8 tall crane
9 lighthouse
10 coal mine (very rare these days)
11 power station
12 monument or obelisk
13 radio tower (usually on top of a hill)
14 windmill
15 small military or civil airport
16 equestrian statue

1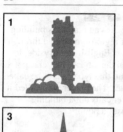

2

3

4

5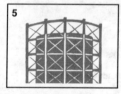

6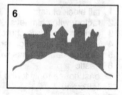

7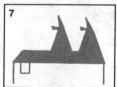

8

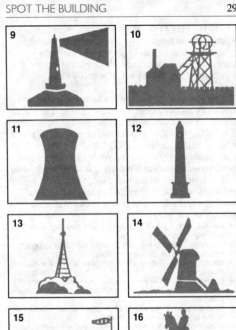

CLOUD SPOTTING ✖

Spotting cloud types is especially fun when travelling
by aeroplane, but it can be played whatever way you
travel; it requires only that each player can see out of a
window and that the sky is not perfectly clear!

Playing

Players agree a time limit beforehand. Each player tries
to identify as many cloud types as possible. The player
to spot the most within the set time limit is the winner.
If travelling by air, remember that planes usually travel
at about 10 000 metres (33 000 feet): using the
illustrations opposite, can you predict what types of
cloud you might see at that height? If travelling by car,
train or boat, can you use the descriptions below to
predict the weather that might be brought on by the
cloud you spotted? Will it rain or snow? Will there be
showers or just drizzle?

 1 **Stratus.** Thin, layered cloud. Patchy and grey. Drizzle
   possible.
 2 **Cumulus.** Separate from others, white and tufted on top and
   dark at the bottom. Showers possible.
 3 **Stratocumulus.** Grey or white, wave-like, and dark in patches.
   Rain unlikely.
 4 **Cumulonimbus.** Tall and tower-like, mixture of white and
   black. Heavy rain, hail or snow possible; thunderstorms also
   possible.
 5 **Nimbostratus.** In a dark and dense layer, sometimes ragged
   on the bottom. Heavy rain or snow likely.
 6 **Altostratus.** In thin sheets, grey or bluish. Rain likely.
 7 **Altocumulus.** Rounded shape, white or grey. Rain likely to
   follow.
 8 **Cirrus.** Thin and wispy, very white and often streaked. Rain
   unlikely.
 9 **Cirrostratus.** Whitish, again wispy, like a smooth veil. Rain
   unlikely.
10 **Cirrocumulus.** Thick, with a grainy texture, and white. Rare.

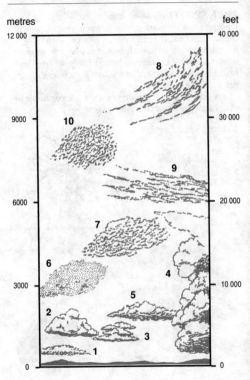

metres | feet

12 000 — 40 000

9000 — 30 000

6000 — 20 000

3000 — 10 000

0 — 0

TREE SPOTTING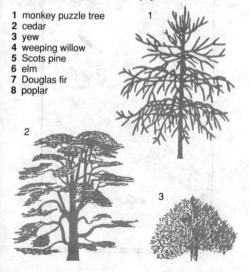

Different tree types have very different shapes, which
you can spot easily even from a distance when
travelling by car or train. It is best to play this game in
winter or autumn, when the foliage has gone from most
trees and the basic shape of the tree is more easily
recognizable.

The winner is the player who first spots an example of
each of the tree types on these pages.

1 monkey puzzle tree
2 cedar
3 yew
4 weeping willow
5 Scots pine
6 elm
7 Douglas fir
8 poplar

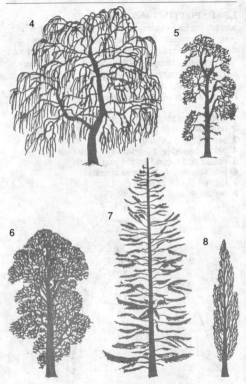

LEAF SPOTTING 🚗 🚄

Identifying leaf shapes can be fun and educational if
your journey takes you to the countryside. Autumn is
the best time to play this spotting game. Players try to
spot as many examples as they can of each of these
different leaf shapes. If possible, when the car or coach
is stopped or the train journey has finished, try to
collect samples of the leaf shapes.

1 smooth and rounded (e.g., alder)
2 heart-shaped (e.g., lime)
3 serrated (e.g., birch)
4 palm-shaped (e.g., sycamore)
5 ribbed and ragged-edged (e.g., oak)
6 five-'fingered' (e.g., horse chestnut)
7 feather-like (e.g., ash)
8 needle-shaped (e.g., pine)

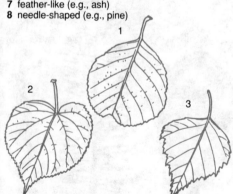

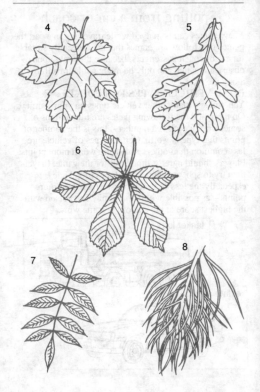

Spotting from a car or coach

Many games can be played while travelling in a car: the games that follow are games that are especially suitable for car or coach passengers, because they rely upon observations that can only be made while travelling along the road.

ROAD VEHICLE TYPES FOR POINTS

You will see many other vehicle types on your journey. On these and the following pages are illustrations of some. Beside each is a number – this is the number of points that type is worth. Certain types of vehicle are less common than others and so are worth more points. Players should agree a time limit for the game. Players then try to spot as many of the types of vehicle – especially the less common ones, which have more points – as possible within that limit. The person with the highest score at the end of the game wins.

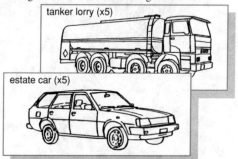

tanker lorry (x5)

estate car (x5)

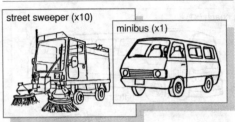

street sweeper (x10)

minibus (x1)

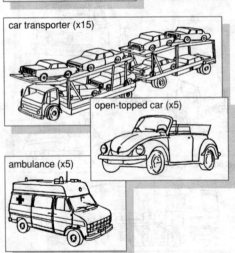

car transporter (x15)

open-topped car (x5)

ambulance (x5)

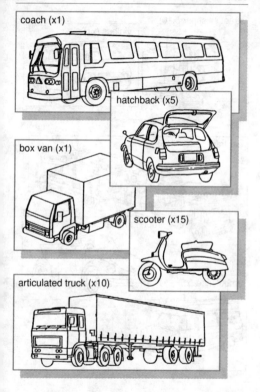

coach (x1)

hatchback (x5)

box van (x1)

scooter (x15)

articulated truck (x10)

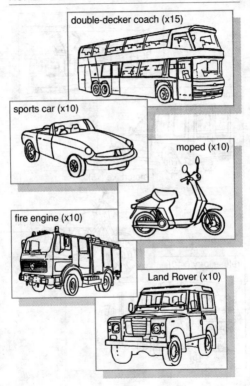

double-decker coach (x15)

sports car (x10)

moped (x10)

fire engine (x10)

Land Rover (x10)

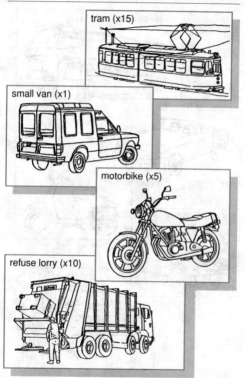

tram (x15)

small van (x1)

motorbike (x5)

refuse lorry (x10)

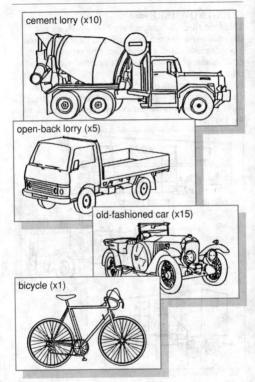

cement lorry (x10)

open-back lorry (x5)

old-fashioned car (x15)

bicycle (x1)

GOING NOWHERE 🚐

There are specially adapted vehicles which are not
intended to move once they arrive at their destination.
These include vans or lorries that convert into shops,
coaches that become libraries or doctors' clinics, and
minibus vans used for camping.

Here are a selection of these mobile vehicles to use as a
guide. Be creative – you may spot others along the
way! The winner is the person who spots the most on
the journey.

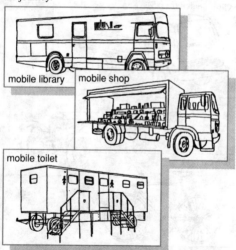

mobile library

mobile shop

mobile toilet

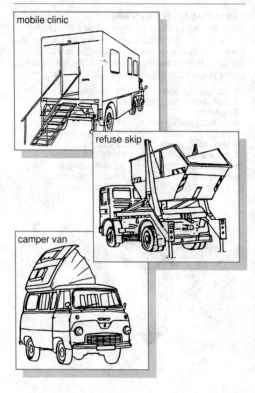

mobile clinic

refuse skip

camper van

PERSONALIZED CARS

Many cars have attachments or special accessories on
their exteriors. In this game, players try to spot as many
of the following attachments as possible; no two
players can count the same object. As you play, add
others you see that are not on the list.

1	car-top luggage carrier	**11**	car badges
2	customized painting	**12**	fog lamps
3	spoilers	**13**	external horn
4	caravan driving mirror	**14**	wide wheels
5	aerial	**15**	sunroof
6	louvred windows	**16**	mascot
7	snow chains	**17**	holiday stickers
8	spot lamp covers	**18**	alloy wheels
9	roof rack	**19**	external exhaust
10	personalized numberplate	**20**	mud flaps

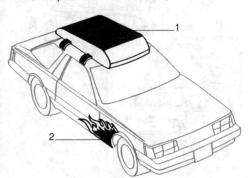

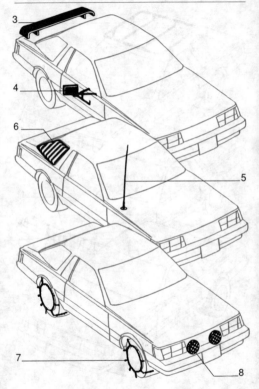

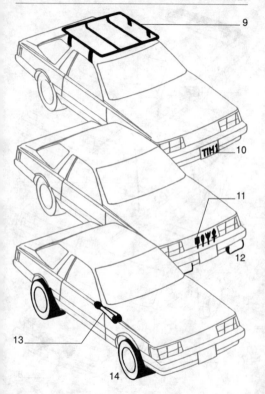

9

10

11

12

13

14

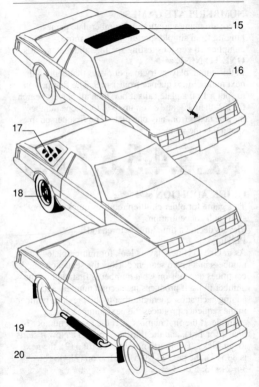

NUMBERPLATE GAMES

There are many variations of numberplate games,
ranging from simple spotting games to more
complicated versions testing spelling and maths skills.

ONE TO NINE 🚗

In this game, players try to spot plates that contain the
next number in sequence from 1 to 9. The first person
to spot a 1 on a plate calls it out, then all players search
for a 2, then a 3, and so on up to 9. Only one number
may be taken from any one plate. The first person to
spot a 9 is the winner.

1.2.3.4.5.6.7.8.9

QUICK ADDITION 🚗

This game for older children requires quick addition
skills and concentration.

Players decide a time limit beforehand.

Playing

As in One to Nine, players look for numberplate
numbers in a given sequence. How the sequence
continues depends on what number is first: adding the
number to itself produces the second number, and
adding each subsequent number to the previous number
in the sequence produces the next number. For
example, if the first number is 1, the second number is
then 2 (or 1+1), and the third is 3 (or 2+1). Now it starts
to get tricky. The fourth number is 5 (or 3+2), the next
is 8 (5+3), the next 13 (8+5), and so on (21=13+8;
34=21+13; 55=34+21).

To make double-digit numbers, simply look for numbers that are adjacent on plates. The number 892, for instance, could be used for 2, 8, 9, 89 or 92.

1,2,3,5,8,13,21

Winning

When the time limit is up, the winner is the player who called out the last number in the sequence.

ALPHA-PLATE 🚗

The rules for this spotting game are the same as for One to Nine, but players look for the letters of the alphabet (in sequence) rather than numbers. The winner is the first player to spot and call out 'Y' (the last letter used on plates).

(Note: You must skip over letters 'I', 'O', and 'Z' – these are not used on numberplates.)

WORD ADD-ON 🚗

In this variation of Alpha-plate, players call out letters they see on numberplates that, when added to the previous letter called out, form a word.

Players should agree beforehand a time limit to the game.

Playing

'A' can be used as the first letter to start the game. Players then look out for a letter that will form a word when added to 'a'. You can add a letter before or after the previous one. For example, a player might spot and call out 'n', forming the word 'an'. Another player might then spot a 'd', forming the word 'and', or an 'm', forming the word 'man'.

A. AN. AND. HAND. HANDY.

Winning the round

The last player to form a word within the time limit
wins that round and chooses a new letter to start with –
e.g., 'o' – for the next round.

SENTENCE ADD-ON 🚗

A variation of Word Add-on in which players look for
letters that will complete a sentence. Instead of a time
limit, players agree beforehand on the sentence, such as
'Spot the letter' or 'What do I see?'.

MAKE A MESSAGE 🚗

A game with no winners, Make a Message can produce
hilarious results. One player spots a numberplate, and
all players create a 'message' out of words that begin
with the letters on the plate, and in that order. The
'message' has to be a sentence – that is, it must include
a noun and verb. A plate with the letters DEP, for
example, could be used to form 'Dogs enjoy playing' or
'Darren eats peas'.

DEP Dogs Enjoy Playing

MAKE THE LONGEST WORD 🚗

This game is a good test of vocabulary for players of all ages.

One player calls out the first three letters on a numberplate – e.g., DEP. All players then take turns trying to form the longest word built on those letters. For example, DEP might be used to form 'depend' or 'departure'.

DEP DEPartmental

QUICK BUILD 🚗

In this game, players look for words in numberplates. When one player calls out a word he or she has spotted, the other players have five seconds in which to call out a longer word based on that word.

ANT

PLANTER CHANTING

FAMOUS NAME FIND 🚗

In this guessing and spotting game, players look for combinations of letters on numberplates which make up the beginning of a famous person's name. One at a time, each player calls out the starting letters, and the other players try to guess the person.

KENNEDY CHAPLIN

NUMBERPLATE BINGO 🚗

Each player needs pencil and paper for this game. One
person agrees to be the caller.

Playing

Everyone draws a large square divided 3 x 3 into nine
smaller squares. In each of their own small squares
players write any two numbers from 0 to 9.

The caller then looks at the numberplates of passing
vehicles and calls out the first two numbers he or she
sees.

Any players with this double-digit number cross it off
their bingo cards. The caller continues to call pairs of
numbers seen on the road.

Bingo cards

73	91	25
11	42	10
22	80	64

player 1

22	19	41
53	27	82
91	47	20

player 2

16	61	48
94	90	88
73	50	32

player 3

Winning

When a player has three numbers crossed off in a row –
across, down or diagonally – that player calls 'Bingo!'
Players then make new cards for themselves and the
caller begins again.

Numbers called

91, 11, 82, 32, 50, 16, 19, 64, 41, 61, 90

player 1   player 2   player 3

73	90	25
11	42	10
22	80	64

22	19	41
53	27	82
91	47	20

16	61	48
94	90	88
73	50	32

number called: 91

number called: 32

number called: 64

number called: 90

player 3 wins

MAKE YOUR NUMBER 🚗

This game can be played individually, in pairs or in a group. It is a good game for older children and for those who enjoy quick mental calculation. Paper and pencil can be used if you wish.

Playing individually

Choose any number from 1 to 50. Then look out of the window and note the three-figure number of the next numberplate you see.

Your aim is to use these three figures to make your chosen number, by adding, subtracting, dividing and multiplying all or some of them.

Suppose your chosen number is 2 and the first numberplate you spot is YGH 375T. You have to make 2 by using 3, 7 and 5. It could be done like this: $3+7=10$, then $10÷5=2$.

Examples

Make 13 from 742
Calculation: $7+4+2=13$

Make 27 from 983
Calculation: $3×9=27$

Make 36 from 195
Calculation: $5-1=4$
                      then $4×9=36$

Make 19 from 415
Calculation: $4+15=19$
                      or $4×5=20$
                      then $20-1=19$

Being adventurous

Sometimes it may seem impossible to make your
number, but by using your numbers in unusual ways
you can find new ideas. For example:

Make 20 from 777
Calculation: 7+7+7=21
              7÷7=1
              then 21-1=**20**

Using larger numbers

Numbers can be chosen from 1 to 100, the larger
numbers sometimes being harder to make. For
example:

Make 69 from 275
Calculation: 2x7=14
              14x5=70
              7-5=2 and 2÷2=1
              then 70-1=**69**

Make 88 from 535
Calculation: 53+5=58
              3x5=15 and 5-3=2
              then 15x2=30
              so 58+30=**88**

Playing in pairs or groups

When two play together, one chooses the number to
make and the other spots a plate number to use. Then
both try to be first to make the number.

When a group of three or more play together, they
agree on a number to make. One person should be
referee by spotting the numberplate and deciding who
made the quickest correct calculation. The winner can
be the next referee.

WHICH CAR? 🚗

This is a simple spotting game, using the colours,
makes or models of cars according to the interest and
knowledge of the players.

Deciding a category

It should be agreed what is going to be spotted:

1 colours of cars – e.g., black, white, green, red, blue,
yellow, grey;

2 makes of cars – e.g., Ford, Nissan, Skoda,
Volkswagen, BMW, Jaguar;

3 models of car – e.g., Metro, Sunny, Granada, Mini,
Riva, Escort.

Playing

Each player chooses one item within the agreed
category, e.g. colours. Then, from an agreed start,
everyone counts how many cars of their colour they
see.

In public transport, counting should be silent. At an
agreed signal, perhaps given by a referee, everyone
compares totals.

Winning

The winner is the one with the highest total.

Variations

Try repeating the game, with everyone exchanging their
chosen colour (or make) of car with another player. In
this way, different players get a chance to win, as there
may be more of one colour of car than another on the
road.

When travelling on a road or motorway, identifying the
type of car depends on the knowledge of the players.
When in a car park these could be identified by the

manufacturers' badges, found on the front of the car.
If you play spotting the makes of cars, take extra care to
look out for other vehicles which may be entering or
leaving the car parking area.
Below and on the following pages are some
manufacturer names and illustrations of car badges:

Audi

Bentley

BMW

Citröen

Honda

Ford

Fiat

Isuzu   Jaguar

Lancia

Land Rover

Lotus

Mercedes-Benz

MG

Mitsubishi

Nissan

Peugeot

Porsche

Renault

Rolls-Royce

Rover

Skoda

Subaru

Toyota

Volvo

Vauxhall

Volkswagen

Yugo

CHILDREN SPOTTING 🚗

Whether your journey takes you through a city or into
small villages, you will see, from your car window,
many other children playing games, going to school or
– like you – watching other children from their car
windows!

How many of the children's activities on these and the
following pages can you spot? Players get one point for
every child. If you are quick enough, you can boost
your score by looking for groups and counting the
number of children in each.

getting an ice cream

BUS

queuing for the bus

rollerskating   skateboarding   cycling

with schoolmates in line

playing in the park

tossing a ball

on a tricycle

with a dog on a lead

playing with a dog

on a swing

ROADWORKS 🚗

When travelling by road for long distances, it is likely that you will come across delays and traffic jams because of road repairs. A good way to while away the time spent in a traffic jam is to observe the people and things involved in work at the roadside.

Each player receives ten points for spotting each of the people, vehicles and machines that are shown on this and the next two pages. The player with the highest score wins.

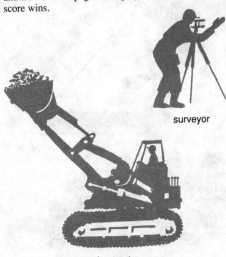

surveyor

excavating tractor

caterpillar crane

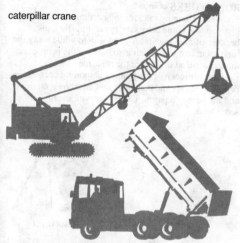

tip-up truck

cement transporter

compactor

dump truck

hydraulic shovel

asphalt layer

PASSING THROUGH THE PAST 🚗

When passing through villages or small towns in a car,
look for monuments that commemorate historical
events, figures or ways of life.
Players receive ten points for spotting each type of
monument shown here on these pages.

war memorial   public fountain

statue of local   sacred site   obelisk
dignitary

tomb

mausoleum

equestrian statue

market cross

Spotting from a train or station

Many games can be played while travelling on a train –
but on the following pages are games that can *only* be
played by train passengers because they rely upon
observations that can usually only be made near a
railway station, on railway platforms or from a train
window.

RAILWAY TYPES

You will see many other types of train on your journey.
On these pages are illustrations of some. See how many
you can spot.

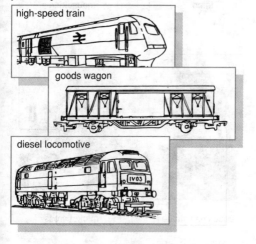

high-speed train

goods wagon

diesel locomotive

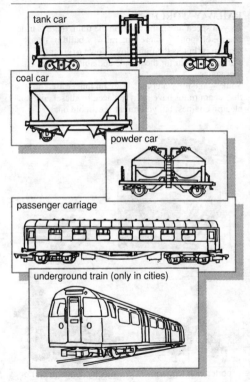

tank car

coal car

powder car

passenger carriage

underground train (only in cities)

RAILWAY WORLD ◢

As you speed down the track on the train, there is little chance of spotting interesting railway buildings and structures, but as the train slows down to enter the station, look out for the people and objects shown on these pages.

Some – like the water tank – are no longer used now that steam trains have been replaced by diesel and electric engines, but you might see an old one.

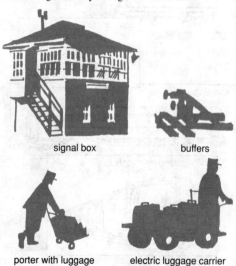

signal box   buffers

porter with luggage   electric luggage carrier

food server

porter without luggage

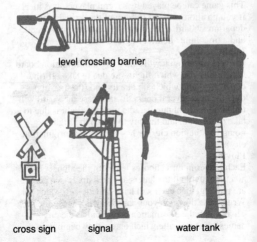

level crossing barrier

cross sign　　　signal　　　water tank

Spotting from a plane or airport

Airports are places in which you might spend a long
time waiting for your flight to be called. They are also
places where you can find a comfortable seat and settle
down to playing lots of the games in this book.
Although many games can be played on an aeroplane
or in an airport, on the following pages are games that
can *only* be played by aeroplane passengers because
they rely upon observations that can usually only be
made near an airport or from an aeroplane window.

FIRST LETTERS ✈

This game can be played by several players. It is ideal
if you position yourself in front of the arrivals and
departures board. Each player needs paper and pencil,
and a time limit should be agreed beforehand.

Flight board

In every airport you will find a flight information board
which tells you which flights are due to take off (the
departures) and which are due to land (the arrivals)
over the next several hours. In each case the board will
tell you the flight number, the time the flight is due to
take off or land, and the city to which the flight is
going (destination city) or has come from (origination
city).

Playing

Each player in turn chooses letters of the alphabet, one
at a time, until all the letters are used up. If two people
are playing, then each will have 13 letters to watch for.
Write these down on your paper as you choose them.
Then watch the information board and as the city
names come up, note which letters they begin with. If

this initial letter is one you have chosen, then tick it off your list.

Players get a point for each letter ticked off their lists. It probably will not be possible to tick off all the letters, so the winner is the person who has the most points after the agreed time period.

COUNTRIES OF ORIGIN ✈

You will need a pocket atlas for this game, which can only be played at international airports.

Again, sitting near the flight information board, look at the flights' origination or destination cities and try to guess which countries the cities are in.

AEROPLANE TYPES ✈

If you can find a place near a large window in the airport looking out onto the runways – or if you have a seat near the window when you board the aeroplane – you may be able to spot many other types of flying vehicles. On the following pages are illustrations of some. See how many you can spot.

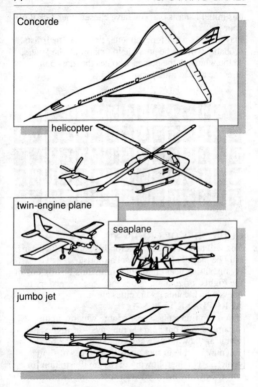

Concorde

helicopter

twin-engine plane

seaplane

jumbo jet

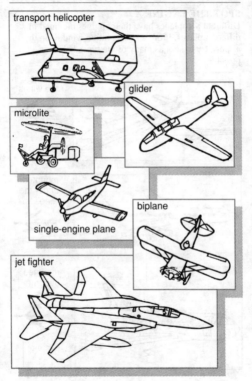

transport helicopter

glider

microlite

single-engine plane

biplane

jet fighter

SPOT THE ENGINE

Different aeroplanes have their engines mounted in different places. From an observation window in the airport, try to spot as many of the types below as possible.

mounted in the wings

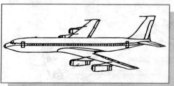

mounted under the wings

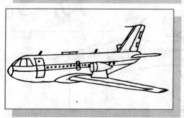

mounted over the wings

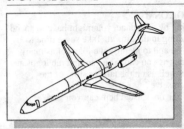

mounted
on the rear
fuselage

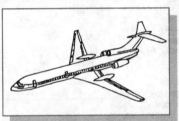

mounted
on the rear
fuselage
and the tail

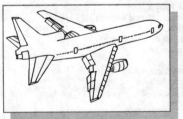

mounted
on the tail
and wings

AIRLINE LOGOS ✈

When travelling by aeroplane, you might have to spend
some time waiting in the airport. Take some time to
look around you and to identify the logos of as many
different airlines as you can. You can find the logos at
ticket desks as well as on the tails or sides of the
aeroplanes themselves.

How many of the ones listed here can you find?

1 Aeroflot
2 Air Canada
3 Air India
4 Air Portugal
5 Alitalia
6 British Airways
7 Cathay Pacific Airways
8 Iberia Airlines
9 Iran Air
10 Japan Airlines
11 KLM (Royal Dutch Airlines)
12 Korean Airlines
13 Lufthansa German Airlines
14 Malaysian Airlines
15 Olympic Airways
16 Pakistan International Airlines
17 Qantas Airways
18 Scandinavian Airlines System
19 Singapore Airlines
20 Swissair
21 Thai Airways International
22 Trans World Airlines
23 United Airlines
24 Virgin Atlantic

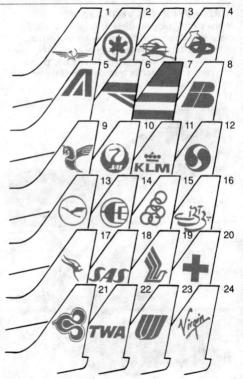

AIRPORT SERVICE VEHICLES ✈

When waiting for your flight departure – or while the
plane is taxiing you to the runway for take-off, try
vehicle spotting. Airport parking bays are always busy
with special vehicles servicing the awaiting planes.
Players get ten points for spotting each of the vehicles
on these and the following pages.

1

2

3

1 **'Follow me in' car.** Guides planes to their parking bay.
2 **Elevated cleaning and servicing truck.** Allows walk-on services to parked planes.
3 **Ground power unit.** Supplies electrical services to stationary planes.
4 **Fire engine.** Kept on stand-by in case of an accident or emergency.
5 **Mobile conveyor belt.** Loads and unloads luggage.
6 **Container convoy.** Supplies pre-stored goods.
7 **Extended services vehicle.** Provides access to wings, engines and the body of the planes.
8 **Fork-lift truck.** For general transportation.
9 **Snow sweeper.** Used to clear snow off the runways.
10 **Mobile lounge.** Elevated access vehicle for passengers.
11 **Tug.** For towing large planes.
12 **Tow truck.** For mooring stranded planes.
13 **Fuel tanker.** For refuelling planes.

4

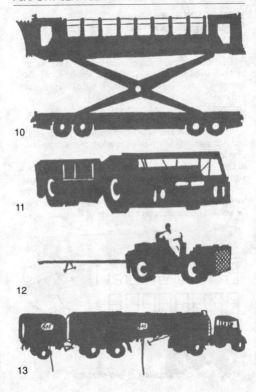

10

11

12

13

JUMBO BINGO ✈

You can play this game when you are on a long air
journey, such as when you are going on holiday.
Seats in new aeroplanes are usually arranged in rows
that have two, three, four, or even five seats across, as
in the case of jumbo jets. The bigger jets have two
gangways travelling their length. The smaller jets have
just one.
Before playing this game, check with the airline
attendant for permission to walk up and down the
gangway. Do not interrupt or annoy other passengers,
and count quietly when moving about the aeroplane.

Playing

In this game for two, both players stand in a gangway at
a point halfway up the rows of seats. One player walks
up towards the front of the plane; the other walks to
the back. As the players walk, they count up how many of
the groups of the seats on either side of the gangway

four possible combinations of two-seat rows

have all males or all females sitting together (do not count children under five years old).

Depending on the layout of the plane, the seats will be grouped in rows of twos, threes, fours, or even fives. Each row of two with all males or all females sitting together is worth two points. A row of three all male or all female passengers is worth three points; a row of four is worth four; and a row of five is worth five.

Winning

Players keep track of their row scores and compare them after each has finished walking up or down the gangway. The person with the highest score wins.

Below are shown the possible combinations of men and women passengers in two-seat rows and three-seat rows. For four- and five-seat rows, there are many possible combinations, so finding a row with all men or all women will be much more difficult.

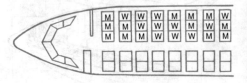

eight possible combinations of three-seat rows

Spotting from a boat or ferry terminal

Many games can be played while travelling on a boat –
but on the following pages are games that can *only* be
played by boat passengers because they rely upon
observations that can usually only be made near a ferry
terminal, ship deck or from another type of boat.

VESSEL TYPES

You will see many other types of boat, either on your
journey or while waiting at the terminal for your
journey to begin. On these pages are illustrations of
some other types of vehicles for travelling on water.
See how many you can spot.

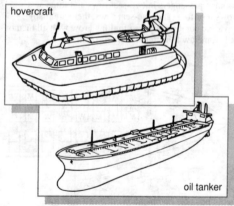

hovercraft

oil tanker

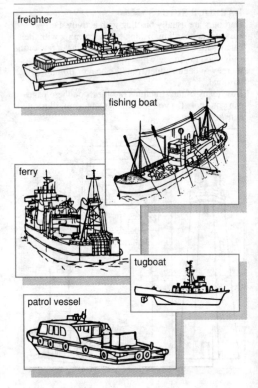

freighter

fishing boat

ferry

tugboat

patrol vessel

HARBOUR SIGHTS 🚢

Harbours are usually bustling with activity. Ferry passengers boarding, fishing boats returning with their catch, sailboats heading out – these are just a few of the sights you might see while waiting for your boat journey to begin, either from the boat or from the terminal.

How many of the structures or objects on these pages can you spot? Do you see others that are not illustrated here?

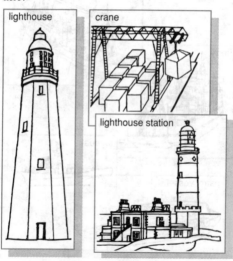

lighthouse

crane

lighthouse station

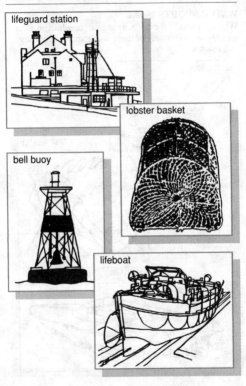

lifeguard station

lobster basket

bell buoy

lifeboat

WATER SPORTS

While waiting in the harbour or port, or while on your journeysee how many of these water sports activities you can spot.

surfboarding

water-skiing

powerboat racing

kayaking

windsurfing

yacht racing

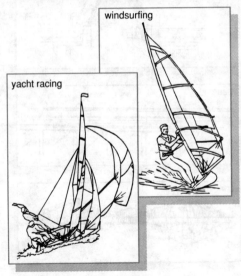

BRIDGE SPOTTING

When in a port – either crossing a river by ferry or setting out on a voyage on an ocean liner – you will probably pass several kinds of bridges. On these pages are six different types of bridge. See how many you can spot. Players collect ten points for each type spotted.

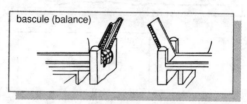

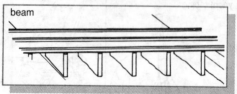

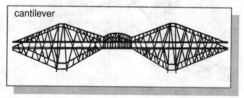

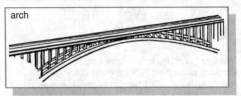

arch

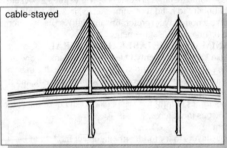

cable-stayed

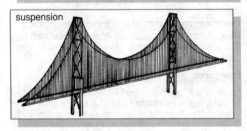

suspension

2. Word and guessing games

Word and guessing games have long been popular forms of amusement. They are especially good when travelling because any number of people can play. In case some disputes arise, it is useful to keep a pocket dictionary to hand. For some games, it is advisable to have a non-player (preferably an adult) acting as referee to resolve any disagreements.

ANIMAL, VEGETABLE OR MINERAL? ✖

Also known as Twenty Questions, this game is one of the oldest and best-known guessing games. It can be as simple or as difficult as players wish to make it, and it can be played in teams or with individual players. It is sometimes helpful for one person to sit out of the game to act as the referee.

Aim

For players to try to identify an object thought of by one of the other players, using only 20 guesses.

Playing

One player thinks of an object. It may be general, e.g. **ship**, or very specific, e.g. 'the deck of the Lusitania'. The player silently decides into which of the following categories his or her object falls.

Categories

animal: all forms of animal life or objects of animal origin, e.g. a centipede, a pearl button, a cow
vegetable: all forms of vegetable life or objects of

vegetable origin, e.g. cotton thread, a wooden chair,
a carrot
mineral: anything of inorganic origin, e.g. a window,
a car, a television set

The chosen objects can belong to a combination of
categories, e.g. a can of beer, a leather shoe with a
rubber sole. In these cases, the player might consult the
referee to help determine which category best describes
the object.

The player indicates the number of words in the object,
excluding 'the', 'a', 'some', etc.

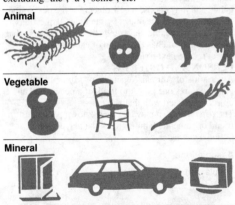

Animal

Vegetable

Mineral

To begin the game, one player asks the first of 20
questions to determine into which category the object
falls. All questions must be answerable with a simple

'Yes', 'No' or 'I don't know'. As such, up to three questions may be required, e.g. 'Is it an animal?', merely to determine the category.

A good strategy is for the guesser to ask questions of a general nature until they feel confident that they are near to identifying the object.

If there is a referee, he or she may intervene if it is suspected that the player has given a wrong or misleading answer.

Winning

The first player to correctly identify the object wins the game, and may choose a new object for the next round.

If no one guesses the object by the time 20 questions have been asked, the player tells the other players what the object is, and has the option of choosing a new object for the next round.

PERSON AND OBJECT ✖

A variation of Animal, Vegetable or Mineral?, this game requires one player to think of a person and an object associated with that person.

The person chosen may be a well-known personality, a friend or someone familiar to all the players, or a fictional character.

Associations

| player 1 | player 2 | player 3 |
| cow → | milk → | cheese → |

Examples

an eskimo and an igloo
Dante and the Inferno
a king and his crown

Playing

The procedure is the same as for Animal, Vegetable or Mineral?, except that players may ask more than 20 questions if necessary.

ASSOCIATIONS ✖

This game requires quick thinking, as the slightest hesitation eliminates a player from the game!

Playing

One player starts by saying any word (preferably a noun), e.g. 'Cow'. As quickly as possible, the next player says the first word that comes to mind, e.g. 'Milk'. The next player in turn then says the first thing that comes to mind, and so on around the group, returning to the first player. Any player who hesitates before saying a word drops out.

Winning

The player who stays in the game longest wins.

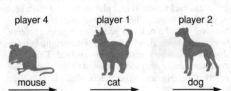

player 4   player 1   player 2

mouse →   cat →   dog →

Association Chains: forwards

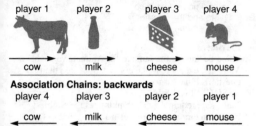

player 1	player 2	player 3	player 4
cow	milk	cheese	mouse

Association Chains: backwards

player 4	player 3	player 2	player 1
cow	milk	cheese	mouse

ASSOCIATION CHAINS ✖

A continuation version of Association can be played
that requires not only quick thinking but a dependable
memory.

Playing

Players go around the group, as in Association, calling
out the first word that comes to mind after a previous
player's word. When the chain has been formed (either
by returning to the first player, or after making several
rounds of the group, depending on the number of
players), the last player to call out a word starts to repeat
the chain backwards. If that player makes a mistake, he
or she drops out and the next player continues to
'unravel' the chain. It is a good idea to have a referee,
who notes down the words used in the original chain, so
that disputes which arise may be resolved. This
continues until either the first word of the chain is
reached, or only one player is left. That player is the
winner.

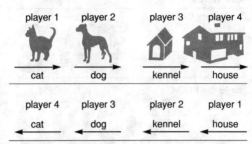

BACK WORDS ✖

This is played like Association. After calling out the next word in the chain the following player must spell it backwards before offering their associated word.

Playing

One player chooses a simple, three-letter word and says it aloud. The other players take turns in trying to spell the word backwards. An example of this game is shown overleaf.

If a player spells the word incorrectly, he or she drops out of the round. A referee making notes of the words would be helpful, in case disputes arise.

Winning

The first player to spell the word correctly backwards wins the round and chooses a word for the next round. The game becomes more challenging if, in each successive round, players choose a word with one more letter than the previous word, e.g. a four-letter word for the second round, then a five-letter word, and so on.

Back Words

three letters **CAT**

TAC

four letters **BOOK**

KOOB

five letters **SHOES**

SEOHS

six letters **POTATO**

OTATOP

BOTTICELLI ✖

This game features well-known people – real or
fictional – and can be both fun and a good test of
general knowledge, but it requires a sensitivity to the
knowledge and level of experience of all players.

Aim

Players try to guess the identity of a person thought of by one player who gives only the first initial as a clue.

Playing

One player thinks of a person or character and tells the other players the initial of that person's surname, e.g. M for Marilyn Monroe.

Taking turns, each player must think of a character whose name begins with that letter, and give a description of him or her without naming the person in mind. For example, one player might ask, 'Are you a Walt Disney cartoon character?'

If the first player recognizes the description (but that character is not the one of which he or she is thinking), that player says, 'No, I am not Mickey Mouse.' Another player then takes a turn guessing the character's identity with a similar question.

If the first player fails to recognize the person being described, or fails to come up with any answer that fits the question – in this case, any Walt Disney character whose surname begins with M – he or she says, 'I don't know.' The player asking the question is then allowed to ask a direct question that will narrow the possibilities and provide a clue. The question must be answerable with a 'Yes' or 'No', e.g. 'Are you in the entertainment business?', and must be answered truthfully.

Winning

The first person to guess the character in mind wins the round, and may choose a new character for the next round.

If no one manages to guess the character after a reasonable length of time, the first player tells the answer and may choose again for the next round.

BUZZ ✘

This game should be played as briskly as possible for maximum enjoyment.

Playing

One player calls out 'One!', the next 'Two!', the next 'Three!', and so on.

As soon as the number 5 is reached – or any multiple of 5 – the player whose turn it is must say 'buzz'. Players must answer immediately.

If the number contains a 5 but is not a multiple of 5, only the part of the number that has a 5 in it is replaced, e.g. 52 would be 'buzz two'.

Buzz

Any player who forgets to say 'buzz' or who hesitates too long drops out of the round.

Winning

The last player in wins the round.

FIZZ ✘

A variation of Buzz, this games requires players to say 'fizz' for every 7 or multiple of 7.

Fizz

5 • 6 • *Fizz* • 8 • 9 • 10 • 11 • 12 • 13 • *Fizz*

BUZZ-FIZZ ✖

This challenging version combines Buzz and Fizz, so that players must say 'buzz' for every 5 or multiple of 5 and 'fizz' for every 7 or multiple of 7, e.g. 57 would be 'buzz-fizz', as would 35.

Buzz-Fizz

1 • 2 • 3 • 4 • *Buzz* • 6 • *Fizz* • 8 • 9 • *Buzz* • 11 •

12 • 13 • *Fizz* *Buzz* • 16 • 17 • 18 • 19

Buzz *Fizz* • 22 • 23 • 24 • *Buzz* • 26 • 27

Fizz • *Buzz* • 31 • 32 • 33 • 34

NEVER SAY IT 🛥 ✈ 🚢

This game requires a book, newspaper or magazine. Each player reads out a paragraph, which has been selected at random, and omits to mention prechosen words. The words should be simple ones such as **and**, **is**, **with** or **on**.

Here is the beginning of the Introduction to this book with **and**, **is**, **for** and **with** omitted. When a player mentions a taboo word they must hand the text over to the next player.

Searching● amusement on a long● boring journey can be frustrating, especially● harassed parents travelling● restless, energetic children.

COFFEEPOT ✖

A simple word substitution game that is easily learned and that can be hilarious.

Playing

One player thinks of a verb. The other players try to guess what it is by asking questions, using the word 'coffeepot' in place of the unknown verb.

For instance, the verb might be **sleep**. Players might search for clues by asking, 'Do you coffeepot with gloves on?' or 'Does everybody coffeepot?'

The first player must respond truthfully with a simple 'Yes', 'No', 'I don't know' or 'Sometimes'.

Winning

The player who correctly guesses the verb is the winner, and they select a verb for the next round.

One-guesser Coffeepot

An alternative version of Coffeepot involves all players but one in deciding on a verb. The player who is the guesser asks questions in order to try to guess the verb. When in a car or other enclosed space, one player writes down a verb on a piece of paper and shows it to the others, while the guesser has his or her eyes closed. As the guesser does not know what the activity is, some of the questions will seem hilarious to the other players.

FOREIGN SHOPPING

A version of charades in which a single item on a shopping list is acted out.

Playing

One player thinks of a typical item on a shopping list. He or she then pretends to be in a shop in which the shopkeepers speak no English; in order to buy the item, the player must act it out.

The other players act as shopkeepers and try to guess what the item is.

Winning

The first person to correctly guess the item is the winner and may have a turn at 'shopping'.

If no one guesses the item, the first player tells the others the answer, and another player is chosen as the shopper.

GHOSTS

This game requires concentration and a good vocabulary.

Playing

One player begins by calling out the first letter of an unstated word. The other players then take turns calling out another letter of a word – either the same word or a different one – taking care not to complete a word. Any player who completes a word 'loses a life', of which each player has three.

For example, the first player might think of the word
about and call out the letter A. The next player then
thinks of a word starting with A which has three or
more letters, e.g. **again**, and calls out the second letter,
G. The next player must call out the third letter of a
word starting with **ag**, e.g. the second A in 'again'. The
next player might then call out 'I'. If the next player is
unable to think of a longer word starting with **agai**, he
or she is forced to call out 'N', completing the word
again and losing a 'life'.

Players can bluff by calling out the next letter of a non-
existent word; if challenged by the other players,
however, the player with the made-up word loses a
'life'. If a player is challenged by another and is able to
come up with an acceptable definition, the challenger
loses a 'life'.

Each player who loses a 'life' becomes a third of a
'ghost'. Losing a second life makes a player two-thirds
of a 'ghost'. Losing three lives means the player has
become a 'ghost' and must drop out of the game.

Winning

The player who survives after all the other players have
become 'ghosts' is the winner of the game.

HOT OR COLD 🚗

A simple guessing game for two or more players.

Playing

One player thinks of an object in or on the car. The
other player tries to guess what the object is, and to
each question, the first player answers 'Hot' or 'Cold',
or something in between, according to whether the
guess is physically near the object.

For example, if the first player is thinking of the

steering wheel, and the second player asks 'Is it the back window?', the first player would respond with 'Cold' or even 'Freezing'. If the guesser asks 'Is it the radio?', the first player would answer 'Warm' or 'Hot'. When the object has been guessed, the second player chooses an object.

I LOVE MY LOVE ✖

In this game, players must think of an adjective, beginning with each letter of the alphabet (in order), to complete a statement.

Playing

One player starts by saying 'I love my love because he (or she) is . . .', completing the sentence with any adjective beginning with the letter A.

The next player repeats the phrase, but this time using an adjective beginning with the letter B. The next player does the same, but using an adjective starting with C, and so on. Players must not hesitate when answering.

Overleaf is a list of adjectives that will be helpful in playing the game.

An alternative version allows players to use a new phrase to continue the game, e.g. 'Her name is . . .', 'She lives in . . . .'

Any player who hesitates or gives a wrong answer must drop out.

Winning

The winner is the last player remaining in the game.

Adjectives for playing I Love My Love

A	attractive, attentive, alluring, appreciative
B	bashful, beautiful, brainy, burlesque
C	charming, cute, courteous, courageous
D	dainty, dextrous, daring, different
E	eccentric, effeminate, errant, extravagant
F	fair, fun, flamboyant, forceful
G	gallant, gorgeous, groovy, generous
H	happy, hilarious, hearty, humble
I	ingenious, illustrious, imaginative, intelligent
J	jaunty, jolly, jubilant, joyful
K	keen, kind, knowledgeable, kooky
L	lenient, loyal, lively, lavish
M	mad, mischievous, modish, mysterious
N	natty, notorious, noble, nice
O	obedient, optimistic, open-minded, outspoken
P	polite, patient, prestigious, profound
Q	quiet, qualitative, queenly, quick
R	rebellious, resolute, resourceful, responsible
S	silly, sagacious, sedate, skilful
T	timid, thin, thoughtful, tolerant
U	upstanding, understanding, unselfish, unflappable
V	voracious, virtuous, vivacious, valiant
W	warm, wholesome, wise, wonderful
X	—
Y	young, youthful
Z	zany, zealous

A WAS AN APPLE PIE ✖

Similar to I Love My Love, players are required to use a verb starting with the appropriate letter of the alphabet instead of an adjective, e.g. 'A was an apple pie. A ate it', 'B baked it', 'C chose it', and so on.

Here is a list of verbs that will be helpful in playing A was an Apple Pie.

Verbs for playing A was an Apple Pie

A	ask, accept, act, address
B	buy, bake, bring, begin
C	catch, choose, cook, change
D	drink, damage, do, dream
E	eat, earn, end, enter
F	find, feel, fetch, feed
G	get, give, giggle, grin
H	hear, hide, help, hit
I	ignore, imagine, imitate, intercept
J	jump, join, judge, juggle
K	kick, know, keep, knock
L	like, learn, light, love
M	meet, make, miss, move
N	need, name, notice, note
O	observe, obtain, occupy, offer
P	Play, post, pass, prepare
Q	quell, quit, quote, queue
R	read, revive, receive, roast
S	sell, speak, scare, send
T	talk, toast, time, test
U	understand, use, uncover, unpack
V	verify, view, visit, vote
W	win, write, want, watch
X	X-ray, xerox
Y	yawn, yell, yank, yield
Z	zap, zone, zip, zoom

HAND GAMES ✖

These are intriguing games of bluff for at least two players, in which each person tries to guess the total number of objects or hand gestures that the other players are concealing under garments layed across their knees, under a table or behind their backs.

Spoof ✘

Each player requires three small objects, such as coins or matches. They hide any number of them (or none if they wish) in their outstretched fists.

One by one, in a clockwise direction, each player calls out the total number of objects they think are contained in the other players' hands – but no two players may say the same number.

When all the players have guessed, they open their fists and the objects are counted. The player who guessed correctly, or whose guess was the nearest to the correct number, wins the round.

Obviously, much depends on the ability to determine whether a player is bluffing when he or she calls a number. For example, guessing high might indicate that the caller has a full hand of three objects (especially if he or she happens to be the first caller in a round).

Similarly, guessing low could mean that a player either has less than three objects in their hand or is attempting to deceive the others about the true number.

The possible combinations that may occur in a game of Spoof, and their values, are shown below and on the following pages. Between two players, the possible totals range from 0 to 6. With three players the values can range from 0 to 9, and so on.

Spoof: possible combinations and their values

total value	player 1	player 2	
0			0+0
1			0+1
			1+0
2			0+2
			1+1
			2+0

total value	player 1	player 2	
3			0+3
			1+2
			2+1
			3+0
4			1+3
			2+2
			3+1

total value	player 1	player 2	
5			2+3
			3+2
6			

Scissors, paper, stone ✖

This game of chance is ancient and is known all over
the world, sometimes under other names such as Hic
Haec Hoc. It is for two players.

Playing

Three objects (scissors, paper and stone) are indicated
by different hand positions:

1 scissors – two fingers making a V shape;
2 paper – an open hand;
3 stone – a clenched fist.

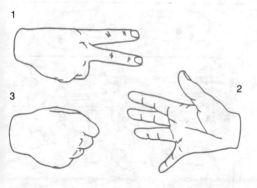

Each player hides one hand behind his or her back and
makes one of the above hand positions. The players call
'One, two, three' (or 'Hic, haec, hoc') together and, on
the third word, each shows the hidden hand in position.

Winning

The relationship of each object to the others decides the winner: scissors can cut paper, paper may be wrapped around stone and a stone can blunt scissors.

Thus, if one player chooses scissors and the other chooses paper, the first player (scissors) wins the round.

A tie is called when both players choose the same hand position.

The game usually continues for a set number of rounds.

Scissors cut paper

Paper wraps stone

Stone blunts scissors

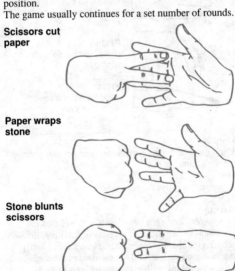

Over the bridge 🚗

If you are travelling by car then Scissors, Paper, Stone can be played with a travel theme. This time the hand gestures represent a car, a bridge and a river.

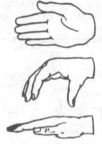

Car
hand held out with the palm facing inwards wins over bridge

Bridge
hand held as an arch wins over river

River
hand held palm down wins over car

Mora ✖

Also known as Fingers, this is another popular hand guessing game.

Aim

Players try to guess the number of fingers that will be shown.

Playing

Two players face each other, each with a closed fist against his or her chest. At a given signal, they 'throw' a chosen number of fingers (or a clenched fist for 0) and, at the same time, call out the total number of fingers they think will be thrown by both of them. A call of 'Mora!' indicates that a player thinks ten

fingers (all five of his or her own and all five of the
other player's) will be thrown.

Winning

The player to guess correctly wins the round. If both
players guess correctly, a tie is called. If neither player
guesses correctly, the round ends with no winner.

A Mora game usually involves 10 or 15 rounds.

Mora: gestures

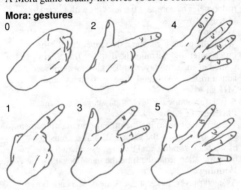

Shoot ✖

A version of Mora, this game requires players to guess
not the number of fingers, but whether the total will be
an odd or even number.

The players may throw the fingers on one or both hands
(for a total of up to 20 fingers).

As they show their hands, the players call out 'Odds!'
or 'Evens!'. The fingers are counted (0 is even), and the
winner is determined as in Mora.

HOW FAR? 🚗

When travelling by car, try this simple game.

Playing

Select a landmark, e.g. the next town, the next
crossroads, the next petrol station. Each person offers a
guess as to the distance to this place (no looking at the
dashboard). The driver, meanwhile, checks the
mileometer to compare the guesses with the true
mileage.

Winning

When the place is reached, the driver checks the
mileometer to determine the distance travelled since the
game began. The player whose guess was closest to the
actual mileage wins and chooses the next game.

MILE! 🚗

A fun, fast game for several passengers in a car.

Playing

The driver, after noting the mileage on the mileometer,
says 'Go', starting the game. All players must look out
of the back window and try to guess when a mile has
been travelled from the time the game began.

Winning

As each player makes a guess, he or she calls out
'Mile!'. After all the players have made their guesses,
the driver declares as winner the player who makes the
most accurate guess.

This is a game which can be played while the players
are engaged in another game and, if combined with
Where's up North (see p. 120), draws the players'
attention to events outside the car.

SPOT ON 🚗

A game of pure chance, this game can be great fun if played by a group of people travelling in a car. Unfortunately, this game is not suitable for wet or snowy weather. Before starting the journey, each player marks with chalk a point on the tyre of the wheel, identifying the mark with an initial or sign. Then, after the journey, when the vehicle has stopped and is securely parked, everyone examines the tyre to see whose mark is closest to the ground. The loser – the person whose mark touches or is nearest the ground – pays a forfeit decided on by the other players.

Spot On

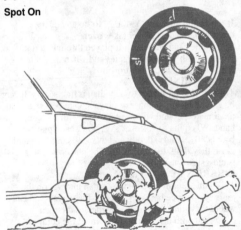

INTERROGATION ✖

Each player takes it in turns to be the 'victim'. The other players ask direct questions related to the journey, the passengers, the places they pass or their destination. Each question must be put so that the easiest answer would be either 'Yes' or 'No'. The victim must answer correctly – but must not use the words 'Yes' or 'No'. Here is an example.

> **Question** Did you pack your tooth brush?
> **Answer** I always do and did so this time.
> **Question** Do you know where we are going?
> **Answer** The destination board said Athens so that's where we will land.

If the victim answers 'Yes' or 'No' to any of the questions, the next player takes over.

This game can be amusing if played throughout the journey, both with other games and when the victim is least expecting to be questioned.

WAIT A MINUTE ✖

This game is far harder to play than it first seems. It can be played by any number of players. One person acts as the timekeeper and will need a watch with a second hand. When the timekeeper says 'Go', each player counts 60 seconds silently and then calls out 'Minute!' when they think the time is up. The player whose guess is closest to one minute wins.

WHERE'S UP NORTH? ✖

This game requires a compass. At an interval on the journey – maybe between games – the players indicate where they think North is. The guesses are then compared with the direction shown on the compass, and the winner is the player who is closest to guessing the correct direction.

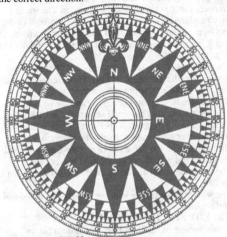

HERE WE ARE ✖

This game helps the players to become better acquainted with their geographical location.

Here We Are requires a compass. It is not as easy as it first seems, particularly if played in the evening or indoors.

When the journey is over and you are unpacking, each person guesses where North is.

The winner is the player whose guess comes closest to the direction indicated by the compass.

SPELLING BEE ✖

One person is chosen as leader, and the other players compete for the title of champion speller. The leader may be given a previously prepared list of words or one can be made up. A watch with a second hand is needed, and it is a good idea to have a dictionary to hand in case disputes arise.

The leader reads out the first word on his list and the first player tries to spell it. He is allowed ten seconds in which to make an attempt at the correct spelling.

If he succeeds, he scores one point and the next word is read out for the next player. If he makes a mistake, the leader reads out the correct spelling; the player does not score for that word (alternatively, the player is eliminated from the game for an incorrect answer), and the next word is read out for the next player.

Play continues until all the words on the list have been spelled.

The winner is the player with the most points at the end of the game.

GREEDY SPELLING BEE ✖

In this version of Spelling Bee, whenever a player spells a word correctly they are given another word to spell. Only when they make a mistake does the next player take a turn, starting with the same incorrectly spelled word. One point is scored for each correct spelling. The player with the highest score at the end of the game wins.

BACKWARDS SPELLING BEE ✖

In this more difficult version of Spelling Bee, players must spell their words backwards. Scoring is the same as in the standard game. If you are travelling by car or

Backwards Spelling Bee

OCIXEM•NILBUD
WOGSALG
NODNOL
NIAPS•AIRTSUA
DNALTOCS
YLATI

plane, it may be interesting to spell place names
selected from an atlas or map.

RIGHT OR WRONG SPELLING BEE

Two teams of equal size need to be formed. Players in
one team are paired with players in the other.

A player chosen as leader calls out a word to each
player in turn, alternating between teams. Each time a
player spells a word, the player with whom he or she is
paired, in the other team, must call out 'right' or
'wrong'. If the second player calls a correctly spelled
word wrong or a misspelled word right, they are
eliminated from the game. Another of the players is
chosen to fill the eliminated player's place.

If the caller makes a correct call, they spell the next
word.

The team that has retained any players wins the game.

HIDDEN VEHICLES ✖

One player selects a single word for a vehicle, such as
ship, **car**, **bus**, **tram** or **bicycle**, and each of the other
players call out words which include the letters of the
word selected. For example, here are ten words which
end in **ship**.

worship, warship, hardship, kinship,
friendship, fellowship, comradeship,
partnership, scholarship, spaceship

WHEELS AND LEGS ✖

Beginning with the letter A, players calls out in turn the
name of a vehicle, continuing in strict alphabetical
order. If a letter occurs for which the next player cannot
think of a vehicle, then an object or an animal with legs
can be selected. If a player fails to think of a word, they
drop out of the game and the round continues without
them.

The winner is the last player to call out a name.

OH 🛶 ✈ 🚤

This game requires careful attention and thought.

Each of the players is selected in turn to read out loud
any page of text from this book.

The reader must speak clearly and slowly.

The other players each take it in turn to listen and call
out 'Oh!' if they think there is an O in the word spoken.

Calling out at an incorrect word, or one without an O,
forfeits a point; calling out at a word with an O earns a
point.

Each player challenges the reader while he or she reads
one page – then it is the next player's turn.

Here is the Introduction to this book. All those words containing one or more Os are printed in bold.

Searching **for** amusement **on** a **long** and **boring journey** can be frustrating, especially **for** harassed parents travelling with restless, energetic children. *Collins Gem Travel Games* is a helpful, exhaustive and highly illustrated **directory to** a variety **of** imaginative games and activities that are suitable **for** playing when travelling. The games (such as **spotting** games, **word** games, quizzes and guessing games) and activities (such as paper **folding**, cat's cradle, making **wool** balls and knitting **on** a **bobbin**) will **occupy those** with enquiring minds as well as **those who** simply **enjoy** playing games **for** their **own** sake. A variety **of** games included here can be swapped **around** regularly **or** played **simultaneously**, **to provide** a greater challenge.

For ease of reference, the games and activities have been listed **according to** their suitability **for** certain types **of** travel, whether by **road**, rail, sea **or** air. Advice is **also** given **on how to** prepare **for** an amusing **journey** and **on** what **to** include in a 'travel pack'.

Created by The Diagram **Group**, *Collins Gem Travel Games* is an attractive **companion volume to** the same team's *Gem Family and Party Games*, *Gem Card Games* and *Gem Games for One*.

INITIAL ANSWERS ✖

A good game for a large group of people.

Playing

One player thinks of a letter of the alphabet, e.g. S, and
a three-letter word beginning with that letter, e.g. **son**.
He or she then gives a definition of the word, starting
with the initial, e.g. 'S plus two letters is a mother's
child.'

The next player tries to guess the word, and then thinks
of a word with four letters also beginning with S, e.g.
soup. That player then gives a definition, e.g. 'S plus
three letters makes a tasty start to a meal.' The next
player guesses and then thinks of a five-letter word
starting with S, and so on.

Any player who fails to think of an appropriate word,
or who fails to guess the previous word, must drop out
of the round.

Winning

The last person left in the game is the winner and he or
she chooses a different letter for the next round.

Initial Answers

three letters	**SON**
four letters	**SOUP**
five letters	**SHEEP**
six letters	**SILVER**

INITIAL LETTERS ✖

A game for several quick-thinking players. A watch with a second hand will be needed.

Playing

One player asks a question – on any subject – that does not require a simple 'yes' or 'no' answer.

Each player in turn must answer the question with two words that begin with his or her initials. Players have only five seconds in which to answer. For example, if the question is 'What is your favourite food?', Bruce Robertson might answer 'Boiled rice.'; Richard Hummerstone might say 'Raw haggis.'; and Carol Dease might say 'Cheese dip.'

When all the players have answered, the second player asks a question, and so on around the group.

Any player who fails to answer after five seconds, or who gives a wrong answer, must drop out of the round. Disagreements about whether an answer qualifies as belonging to the chosen category should be decided by a referee.

Initial Letters

Bruce	**Robertson**
Boiled	**Rice**
Carol	**Dease**
Cheese	**Dip**

I WENT ON A TRIP ✖

This game is a good test of memory skills, as players try to remember and repeat a growing list of items.

Playing

One player chooses an article, e.g. umbrella, and begins the game by saying, 'I went on a trip and took my umbrella.'

The next player repeats that sentence and adds a second article, e.g. 'I went on a trip and took my umbrella and my dog.'

The game continues around the group, each player repeating the previous sentence and adding another article, so that gradually a long list is built up.

I Met a Mongoose

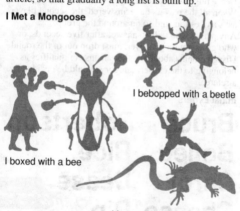

I bebopped with a beetle

I boxed with a bee

I leaped over a lizard

Whenever a player cannot remember the list correctly, the round is over and the next player in the group begins a new list.

I MET A MONGOOSE ✖

This game is similar to I Went on a Trip. This time each player chooses an animal and an activity, both of which begin with the same letter of the alphabet or which have the same sound at the beginning. For example, 'I carried a kangaroo' or 'I kept a cat'. The fun lies in inventing phrases that involve unlikely activities with unlikely creatures.

I organized an ostrich race

I led a llama

I DROVE A DUMPER ✖

This is a similar game to I Went on a Trip, but this time each player selects a method of travel to a destination with an initial letter which is the same as that of the vehicle chosen. Many of the illustrations in this book may help you to think of means of transport.

I Drove a Dumper

I skateboarded to Skegness

I glided to Glasgow

I canoed to Cairo

LAST AND FIRST ✖

Also called Chain or Grab on Behind, this fast-moving
game is ideal for several players.

Playing

Players decide on a specific category, e.g. flowers,
people, food.

The first player calls out a word in the chosen category,
e.g. **cheese**. The next player in turn calls out another
word, in the same category, that begins with the last
letter of the first word, e.g. **egg**.

Play continues in this way around the group, with each
player having only five seconds in which to call out a
word.

Words cannot be repeated once they have been used,
and any player failing to call out a word in time (or
calling out an incorrect word) drops out of the round.
Any disagreements, about whether an answer qualifies
as an item in the chosen category, should be decided by
a referee.

Winning

The last player to stay in wins the round, and a new
round is played.

Last and First

CHEESE EGG GRAPES
SAUSAGES SALAD
DUCK KEBAB B . . . .

LOST VOWELS ✖

A word game that is much more challenging than it appears.

Playing

One player thinks of a word – preferably one with many vowels – and says it aloud but leaving out all the vowels. For instance, **rough** would become **rgh**.

The other players try to guess the word, either the same word the first player is thinking of, or a different word that uses the same consonants in the same order. For example, **right** would not be a correct guess because it has a T in it, which **rough** does not have. If the first player were thinking of **mall**, and said 'Mll', acceptable guesses would be **mill** and **mull**.

Winning

The first player to guess correctly wins and takes a turn choosing a word.

Lost Vowels

group of letters	possible answers
dg	**dig dog dug**
rgh	**rough**
trgh	**trough**
strght	**straight**

MISSING VOWELS ✖

A game in which vowels are left out of the alphabet.

Playing

Each player takes a turn. The first recites the alphabet omitting the vowels; should they complete it without a mistake, they then repeat the alphabet backwards omitting the vowels. Should a mistake be made, the player drops out and the next player takes over.

Winning

The last player to stay in the game wins.

Here is the alphabet printed backwards. It may prove helpful when playing the game.

ZYXWVUTSRQPONMLKJIHGFEDCBA

SILENT BEGINNINGS ✘

Also known as Never say the Start. It is similar to Lost Vowels, but in this instance the player who leads says a word without pronouncing the first letter.

Playing

Players start off with a set number of points, e.g. 10 points.

One player thinks of a word, preferably one with an ending similar to other words, e.g. **sing**. They then say the word, omitting the first letter, e.g. '–ing'. The other players must then call out in turn a word ending in the same spoken letters, but they must add a letter to the front. They might call out 'King!' or 'Ring!'. A point is lost, however, for every wrongly guessed word.

The player who calls out the correct word takes a turn at choosing a new word ending.

Winning

The player with the most points at the end of the game wins.

ONE MINUTE PLEASE ✖

This game calls for quick wits and a free imagination.

Aim

Players try to speak on an assigned subject for one minute. One player sits out to act as referee and to assign the topics.

Playing

Each player in turn is given a topic. It can be anything from a serious subject, such as 'the current political situation', to something silly, e.g. 'why children like sweets'.

The subject may be treated in any way the player likes, and they may even talk utter nonsense, providing he or she does not deviate from the topic, hesitate too long or repeat things.

Other players may challenge the speaker if they feel that any rules have been broken.

Winning

The player who manages to speak for one minute wins the game. If two players succeed, the winner is decided by a vote on which speech was best or by another round.

READ MY LIPS 🍫 ✈ 🚢

A good game for young children, and for any number of players.

Aim

To guess the words mouthed by one player.

Playing

One player faces the others and silently mouths the words to a line of a well-known poem or song. The other players try to guess the words.

Winning

The first player to guess the entire line is the winner. He or she then takes a turn at mouthing a sentence.

TRAVELLER'S ALPHABET ✖

A challenging word game with sometimes hilarious results.

Playing

The first player must pick a destination beginning with the letter A and say, e.g. 'I am going on a journey to Amsterdam.'

The next person then asks, 'What will you do there?' The answer the first player gives must use a verb, an adjective and a noun, all beginning with A, e.g. 'I shall acquire attractive antiques.'

The second player must then give a destination beginning with the letter B and, when asked, respond with a statement using a verb, an adjective and a noun, all beginning with B.

The game continues in this way around the group, going through the entire alphabet if possible.

Any player who cannot respond drops out of the game. A more challenging alternative is for players to link their responses to the destination, e.g. 'I am going on a journey to Greece . . . to guzzle gorgeous grapes.'

Any player can be challenged by another player. If the challenged player cannot think of a more suitable phrase, he or she drops out. If, however, the phrase is found to be suitably linked, the challenger must drop out.

Winning

The last player remaining in the game is the winner.

TOWN ENDINGS 🚗

A game requiring a road atlas. One player looks in the index of a road atlas and selects the name of a place which ends in **ing**, **kirk**, **by**, **ford** or **mouth**.

They then challenge the other players to guess the name of the place selected. Whoever guesses correctly then takes a turn searching the index for a new place name.

WHAT'S MY NAME? ✖

This is a fairly simple game in which one player does all the guessing.

Playing

One player is chosen as the guesser and closes his or her eyes while one of the other players chooses a well-known personality – real or fictional, dead or alive – and writes the name down for the others to see.

When they have finished (and the paper on which the name is written has been hidden), the guesser opens his or her eyes and asks, 'Who am I?' The other players each reply with a clue to the character's identity. For example, if the character is Napoleon, answers to the question might be

> you are rather short and stout
> you are a great strategist at war
> you underestimated the Russian winter

When each of the players has given one reply, the guesser has three chances to identify the character. If the player cannot guess the character, he or she is told the answer, and another player is chosen to be the guesser for the next round.

WHERE AM I GOING? ✖

Played like What's My Name?, but this time the players

select a place somewhere in the country or the world.
The guesser must then ask 'Where am I going?', and
the replies may be descriptive.

    you are going to a very hot place
    you can go there by camel
    there is lots of sand
    there is no beach

Alternatively, letters of the place name can be revealed.

    it has two Ts
    U will end up here

The place intended is Timbuktu!

DESTINATIONS ✘

This game can be played using an atlas which features
the major towns and cities of the British Isles. Should
the destination be a foreign country, then a map of that
country would help to familiarize the players with their
destination.

Playing

One player begins by naming a place on the map, e.g.
Glasgow. The second player then names a place which
begins with either the last or the first letter of the
previous place; in this case, a place beginning with
either G or W, e.g. Worcester. The third player must
then (if there are more than two players) mention a
place beginning with either W or R.

The game continues until a player is unable to think of
a place, or they mention a place previously named. In
either case, the player concerned drops out.

GLASGOW WORCESTER ROCHESTER RYE

Winning

The winner is the last player to remain in the game.

STORY WHEEL ✘

A story wheel is made up of a series of card circles that have elements of a story written on them. The circles are turned individually to give different combinations of words and phrases. Participants then take turns to make up a story using the elements that have been selected.

The story wheel is best made before a journey is started. It can also be made whilst waiting at an airport or station, for example. As scissors are needed for making the wheel, it should not be made in a moving vehicle.

Making the story wheel

You will need:

1 five sheets of plain, thin card or plain, strong paper measuring about 25 cm (10 in.) across;

2 scissors;

3 a wing clasp for securing the story wheel;

4 a pen.

A paper story wheel will not last as long as a card one.

1 Cut out five circles from the paper or card. They should have the following diameters (given in centimetres and inches):

a 10 cm (4 in.);

b 13.5 cm (5½ in.);

c 17 cm (7 in.);

d 20.5 cm (8½ in.);

e 25 cm (10 in.).

1

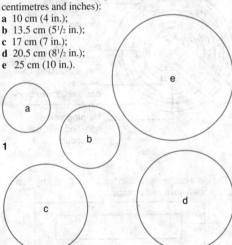

2 Write helping verbs, nouns, adjectives, action verbs and phrases on the edges of the card circles. Some examples are shown here.

2

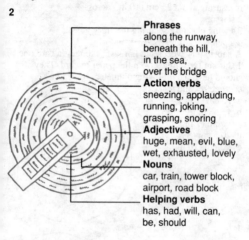

Phrases
along the runway,
beneath the hill,
in the sea,
over the bridge

Action verbs
sneezing, applauding,
running, joking,
grasping, snoring

Adjectives
huge, mean, evil, blue,
wet, exhausted, lovely

Nouns
car, train, tower block,
airport, road block

Helping verbs
has, had, will, can,
be, should

3 Cut out a rectangle measuring 17 cm (7 in.) by 5 cm (2 in.), with a slit in the centre.

3

4 With the marked sides of the circles facing upwards, place each of the circles on top of each other, the largest at the bottom and the smallest on top, and add the rectangle. Fasten them together with the clip.

4

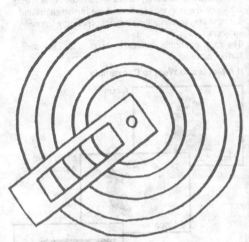

Once the story wheel has been made, participants are able to take it in turns to rotate the circles at random, and the words that appear within the rectangle must be used by another player to create a story.

IF A MET B AND WENT TO C ✖

Here is a game requiring imagination and storytelling skills. A player selects one item from each of the following three pages, and the next player has to weave a story around the three items selected. Pictures might be chosen, e.g. of a nun, Africa and a train. After telling the story, the storyteller selects three further items and the next player retells the story incorporating the new subjects.

The game continues with each player in turn selecting further entries.

If A Met B and Went to C: example

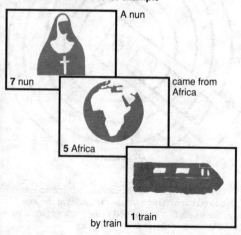

If A Met B and Went to C: people

1 clown

2 business man

3 punk

4 photographer

5 jogger

6 soldier

7 nun

8 chef

If A Met B and Went to C: types of transport

1 train

2 truck

3 bus

4 car

5 bicycle

6 motorcycle

7 boat

8 aeroplane

If A Met B and Went to C: places

1 home

2 theatre

3 castle

4 desert island

5 Africa

6 around the world

7 the countryside

8 the city

ANIMAL FAMILIES ✖

A game in which one player selects animals from the list below and another has to recall the correct name for the male or female of the species. After guessing the names of ten animals, the players swap roles and the second player calls out the name for the animal's young.

Animal	Male	Female
deer	buck	doe
hare	buck	doe
bear	bear	she-bear
fox	fox	vixen
pig	boar	sow
goat	billy	nanny
donkey	donkey	jennet
dog	dog	bitch
sheep	ram	ewe
horse	stallion	mare
cattle	bull	cow
seal	bull	cow
goose	gander	goose
duck	drake	duck
other types of bird	cock	hen

WHAT'S THE WORD FOR IT? ✖

Each player takes it in turn to select entries from any of
the five lists below and asks, for example:

What is a male . . . called?
What is a baby . . . called?
What is the female name for . . . ?
What is the name for a collection of . . . ?

Young	Group
fawn	herd/leash
leveret	down/drove/husk/lie/trip
cub	sloth
cub	earth/lead/skulk
piglet	litter/herd/sounder
kid	flock/herd/tribe/trippe
foal	herd/drove
puppy	cowardice/kennel/pack
lamb	down/drove/flock/hurtle
foal	herd/stable/stud/troop
calf	drove/herd
pup	harem/herd/pod/rookery
gosling	gaggle/flock/skein/plump
duckling	mob/sail/badeling
chick	congregation/flight/flock

3. Pencil and paper games

For all these games a pencil or pen and some paper will
be needed. A small pad of paper with a cardboard base
is handy for writing on where a floor or table cannot be
used. Thin card is very useful, such as the backs of old
greetings cards or card cut from cereal boxes.

SENTENCES FROM WORDS

There are both easy and challenging ways of playing
this game. It can be played alone or players can work
out solutions in pairs or groups.

Playing

Choose a word containing five to seven letters and
write it down, e.g. **where**, **castle** or **animals**. It may be
helpful (if no appropriate ones can be thought of) to
pick words out of a newspaper or magazine.

The aim is to use each letter of the chosen word to form
a sentence. Any kind of nonsense will do, providing all
the letters are used in the order in which they appear, as
in these examples.

Sentences from Words

WHERE	CASTLE	ANIMALS
Winnie	**C**rumpled	**A**ll
Hates	**A**ging	**N**ew
Empty	**S**nails	**I**slands
Red	**T**orment	**M**ake
Eyes	**L**ittle	**A**
	Ethel	**L**ong
		Sunset

Cooperating

Pairs and groups of players can join forces to make sentences from longer words such as

HIPPOPOTAMUS

Possible words	**Possible sentence**
Harry, hungry, hiccup	**How**
India, interior, igloo	**Is**
picking, Peter, pool	**Peter**
pole, paint, pathetic	**Potts**
outside, on, opal	**Opening**
polo, pair, pineapple	**Pink**
orange, ostrich, over	**Oysters**
Tim, tiny, toddler	**Then**
Argentina, apricot, all	**Arguing**
mammoth, magic, mug	**Music**
under, umbrella, ugly	**Up**
sad, sorry, Spain	**Stairs?**

Competing

An element of competition can be introduced if each player makes a sentence from the same word. The first player to make a sentence wins. For example:

LETTER

Lower Ernest To The End Rung

Let Edna Touch Two Early Racoons

A challenge

Try to make sentences from all the letters of the
alphabet in order. Start new sentences when one cannot
be taken any further. The sentences do not have to
make sense either separately or together.

A,B,C,D,E,F,G,H,I,J,K,L,M,N,O,P,Q,R,S . . .
A Big Crow Danced Endlessly For George. How Is
Jack Keeping? Leap More Nimbly Over Peter's Quaint
Red Socks . . . and so on.

Can you use every letter of the alphabet, in order, in
one long sentence of 26 words? Or make a set of
sentences that are linked?

A B C D E F G H I J K L M N O P Q R S T U V W X Y Z

One way to make a continuous sentence is to include a
list of things, for example:

Aunt Betty's Cuddly Dog Eats Flies, Green Honey In
Jars, Kinky Lupins Made Near Oz, Peeled Quinces,
Raw Sausages, Tinned Umbrellas, Very Wavy Xmas
Yoyos, (and) Zips!

WORD ENDINGS

A good game for any number of players who like words
and can spell reasonably well!
It is helpful if each person is referee in turn, although
they can still take part in the game.

Playing

First one subject is chosen. The subject can be broad,
e.g. animals. This is better for younger children. For
older children, the subject could be limited to, say,
mammals or even to mammals that live in the country

through which you are travelling. Here are some
examples of subjects:

animals	cities	bulbs	books
plants	streets	capitals	plays
countries	colours	cars	films
towns	metals	comics	computers
shapes	pop songs	sports	badges
transport	food	seas	rivers
mammals	airports	drinks	
flowers	birds	clothes	

characters from history, cartoon characters,
TV characters, TV programmes, place names

When a subject has been chosen, the referee chooses
one letter.
Then everyone writes down their own words, connected
with the subject, and which end with the chosen letter.
Here are some examples:

subject	letter	sample words
shapes	E	square, circle
birds	N	robin, pigeon
food	R	butter, hamburger
sports	G	running, swimming

Winning

After an agreed time, each player reads out their list.
Everyone ticks any words on their lists that are the
same as those read out by the other players. One point
is scored for each word which is the same as someone
else's. Two points are scored for each word that nobody
else has found. Players note their scores. The one with
the most points is the winner and becomes the referee
for the next game, when a new subject and a new letter

are chosen. Subjects may be repeated, but a different
letter should be used.

Variation

This version takes longer. Everyone writes down the
same list of topics in a column on the left-hand side of a
piece of paper. A letter is agreed; each person writes
down a word for each subject, ending in that letter. To
score, players read out their lists of words in turn as the
others tick any words that they have that are the same.
One point is scored for a correct word that is the same
as someone else's, and two points are scored for a word
that nobody else chooses. In the example below, the
chosen letter is N and there are four players.

How to score

subjects	John	Jenny	Simon	Maureen
animals	chicken	fawn	chicken	hen
towns	Bolton	London	London	London
colours	green	brown	green	brown
sky	sun	sun	moon	rain
scores	1+2+1+1	2+1+1+1	1+1+1+2	2+1+1+2
totals	= 5	= 5	= 5	= 6

Maureen is the winner.

CONGLOMERATION 🛬 ✈ 🚢

A quiet game of concentration and ingenuity for any
number of people who enjoy word puzzles.

Playing

The word **conglomeration** is written by all the players
in capital letters across the top of their papers.

CONGLOMERATION

The aim of the game is to make as many words as possible using the letters of this keyword.

A time limit of, say, 15 minutes might be agreed.

It is a good idea to write the words in lists, according to how long they are, e.g. three-letter words, four-letter words, five-letter words, and so on.

Rules

Letters can be used only as often as they occur.

Letters occurring once, such as A and E, can be used only once. There are three Os and two Ns, so words that use two or three Os or two Ns can be made.

The letters can be used in any order.

Any kind of word can be made that is in common use, except proper names, such as **Colin** or **Nile**.

Winning

The person with the longest list of correct words is the winner. Players can exchange lists to check if there are any doubtful words. If there are, a vote should be taken as to whether they may be included or not.

Changing the keyword

The winner of the game may choose a new keyword. Any long word can be used.

Conglomeration: other keywords

DISINTEGRATION
UNFORGIVABLE
ROMANTICALLY

Shorter keywords, such as those below, offer a greater
challenge.

TECHNIQUE
THEATRE
MONSTER
ANSWER

A longer game

Another way to play this game is to take groups of
words, e.g. the days of the week, the names of the first
six months of the year, the names of the players or the
last four place names passed on your travels. Then
make words from each keyword in the group in turn.

Scoring

The score is equal to the number of words made. In the
longer game, there will be winners for each keyword in
the group. For example, if the keywords are the days of
the week, there will be a Monday winner, a Tuesday
winner, and so on. Finally, all scores are added together
to find the overall winner.

A variation for quick thinkers

Any common saying or quotation, or the words of a
short rhyme or song, can be used to make other words
from each word in the phrase.

> a rolling stone gathers no moss
> nothing ventured nothing gained
> what goes around comes around
> you can't make a silk purse from a sow's ear

ALL CHANGE

This game can be played alone or in competition with others. Quick thinking and good spelling are needed to win.

The aim is to change one word into another of the same length, using a chain of words.

For example, to change **head** into **tail**, four link words are needed. Each link word is made by changing only one letter of the word before it, as shown below. The link words must be in the dictionary. Proper names and abbreviations are not allowed.

All Change

H	E	A	D
H	E	A	L
T	E	A	L
T	E	L	L
T	A	L	L
T	A	I	L

Playing

Two words of the same length are chosen and written down. Everyone tries to make a chain.

Scoring

The first to finish calls out. If everyone agrees that the chain is accurate, that player scores one point. If two or more people call out at the same time, the one with the least number of link words gets the point.

The winner then selects the next two words.

Below are some examples. Some may need long chains to change the first word into the second.

Some pairs of words to change

WHITE into BLACK
BOY into MAN
HAND into FOOT
LARGE into SMALL
WIND into RAIN
FOUR into FIVE
REACH into TABLE

Any two words can be chosen providing they have the same number of letters. Occasionally, it may be impossible to continue a chain, so nobody scores.

NOUN GROUPS ✈ ⛴

This game can be played alone or in competition with others. For instance, a pair of players can challenge another pair.

Preparing

Any word with six different letters is chosen, e.g. **answer**, **scream** and **lights**.

The chosen word is written at the top of the paper. The letters of the word are written vertically down the left-hand side of the page, with possible noun-group categories written across the top.

Playing

The aim is to use the letter at the left-hand side of each row as the initial letter of the nouns in the groups.
The columns can be filled in as words come to mind.

Noun Groups: example

PRANCE

	CAR	PLACE	ANIMAL	FOOD
P	PEUGEOT	PARIS	PIG	PIE
R	ROVER	RUSSIA	RAT	
A		ARABIA	ANT	APPLE
N	NISSAN	NIGERIA		NUT
C		CHESTER	CON	CHIPS
E		EIRE	EWE	EGG

Winning

When playing alone, it is a good idea to set a time limit.
When competing, the first person or group to finish is the winner, providing everyone agrees their list is correct. If not, the next best scores the winning point.
The winners choose the next six-letter word and the losers choose the categories, which can be the same as before.

WORLD GEOGRAPHY 🚢 ✈ 🚤

A simpler version of Noun Groups, only one letter and one subject are used. Players compete with each other.

Preparing

A non-playing timekeeper will be needed, or all the players can synchronize their watches and agree a finishing time. Five to ten minutes will be enough time.

A letter is chosen. This can be done by a non-player or by using this book:

1 one player holds the book;

2 the next player picks a page number, e.g. p. 79;

3 the next player picks a line number, e.g. line 13;

4 finally, a number for a word is chosen, e.g. 5;

5 the player with the book would look for the fifth word in line 13, on p. 79;

6 the first letter of that word is used for the game.

Playing

When the letter is chosen, the game begins and each player writes down, on their own paper, words connected with world geography that begin with the letter. For example, if the letter F had been chosen the list might look like this:

Farming	**Fog**
Fault	**Fossil**
Fjord	**Freeze-thaw**
Floodplain	**Florence**
Fertilizer	**Finland**
France	**Fish-farming**
Forests	**Fords**
Floods	**Florida**

The aim is to think of as many words as possible in the given time.

Scoring

When the time is up, one player reads out their list and the others check theirs. Then the next player reads out any words not already mentioned, and so on.

Players get one point for words also chosen by someone else and two points for words nobody else has written down.

The player with the highest score is the winner.

Other subjects

Broad subjects should be chosen, such as those given below.

animals that live on land
first names, male
first names, female
flowering plants
mechanical transport
items of clothing
sports of the world

Subjects can be repeated using a different letter.

NAME A LIST

A name-searching game for one or more players.

Preparing

Players write the same list, of about 16 subjects, in a column down the left-hand side of their pieces of paper. The list of subjects can be used more than once or can be replaced by an entirely different one.

Below are possible lists of subjects.

list one	list two	list three
mammal	city	book
reptile	state	nursery rhyme
fish	country	author
bird	town	poet
insect	province	politician
vegetable	village	singer
flower	pub	composer
fruit	hotel	pop group
nut	airport	artist
grain	girl's name	cartoonist
seed	boy's name	TV game
tree	surname	TV character
river	royal person	TV soap
mountain	footballer	film/video
lake	sportswoman	play/musical
sea	sports arena	DIY tool

Playing

When the list is ready, a letter is chosen and everyone writes a name for everything on the list that starts with that letter.

When five minutes are up, the names are checked by one player at a time reading out their list until all the names are checked.

Five rounds are played using the same list.

Scoring

One point is scored for every name that is agreed to be correct and that someone else has written. Two points are given for names that nobody else has written, as long as they are correct.

Winning

The winner of a round is the person with the highest number of points for that round. The winning player chooses the letter for the next round.

When five rounds have been played, everyone totals their scores for all the rounds. The overall winner is the player with the highest score.

If the game is to continue, the overall winner chooses the next list of subjects for another five rounds. New letters are chosen as before.

FILL THE GAP

A game for three or more players, who challenge each other in turn to find words that contain three given letters.

Playing

Each player takes a turn at being the challenger and to time the others. Five minutes should be allowed.

The challenger gives the players three letters and challenges them to find words in which the letters all appear in a given order.

The best way to pick letters is to think of any word, e.g. **letter**, and to use three letters from it, e.g. L, T and E.

Fill the Gap: examples

BLANKETTED	FLUSTER	LUTE
BLOATER	FLUTE	PLATE
CLOTTED	LATE	PLOTTED
CLUSTERED	LATRINE	POLITE
	LETTER	

It is easier to compare words if they are in alphabetical order.

Scoring

The challenger stops the game after five minutes and
takes the lists to check, marking those that are correct.
The players then count up the number they have correct
and that becomes their score for the first round.
The next player becomes the challenger and chooses
another set of letters for the second round.
The game continues until all the players have
challenged each other.

Winning

Each player totals their scores for each round. The one
with the highest overall total is the winner.

ANAGRAM CHALLENGE 🛥 ✈ 🚢

This is a game where two people or teams can compete
with each other. It is a game for players who really
enjoy letter puzzles and are good with words.

Sample anagrams

An anagram is a new word or phrase that is made by
rearranging the letters of another word or phrase. For
example: **late** rearranged becomes **tale**; **medication**
becomes **decimation**; **salesmen** can be rearranged to
make **lameness**, **maleness** and **nameless**; **disgustedly**
will make **Sid glued sty**; and **assistant** makes **Stan is
sat**.

Preparing to play

Players split into two groups, which will play against
each other.
Each group has to think of a set of ten anagrams, which
are then written on a piece of paper. The first five
should be single words that make other words. The rest
should be single words that make phrases.
A separate list of the ten answers to the anagrams have

to be made, so that each team can compare the other's answers with its own.

A time limit, within which to solve the anagrams, is agreed.

Playing

When the lists are ready, the groups exchange papers and the contest begins to find the anagrams.

A non-playing timekeeper should call out when the time limit is reached, e.g. after five minutes.

Winning

Groups exchange papers for checking. The first group to have correctly solved the most anagrams in the given time wins. If an anagram is found that is not the same as that given by a challenger, it still counts.

SQUARED WORDS

This game can be played individually or competitively with two or more players.

Preparing

Draw five vertical lines and five horizontal lines to make a large four-by-four square.

Playing

In one of the horizontal rows write any word of four letters, e.g. **lane**.

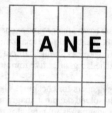

Then try to complete the square so that there are four words across and four words down.

Across
spit
lane
arks
pest

Down
slap
pare
inks
test

S	P	I	T
L	A	N	E
A	R	K	S
P	E	S	T

Another square challenge

Make a word square with the same four words across as down. It is an idea to make the diagonals into words as well or to try some larger squares.

PYRAMID WORDS

Each player has a pyramid, like the one below, and they fill in a sentence that reads from top to bottom: each word has more letters in it than the proceeding word. To really test everyone's imagination, add more rows until a sentence has been created in which the last word has eleven, or even thirteen, letters.

Pyramid Words

CROSSWORD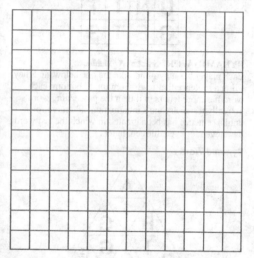

A progression from Squared Words, this game can be
played individually or in groups.

Preparing

A grid with 12 squares across and 12 down is needed.

Playing

Each player in turn calls out one letter. Everyone writes
them down until 25 letters have been called. The same
letter can be called more than once.

ENTEESIDRINOP
YAPSXTBULQMZ

The aim is then to build complete words across and down, filling in squares between the words, as shown in the example below.

As each of the 25 letters are used, they should be crossed out so that they cannot be used again.

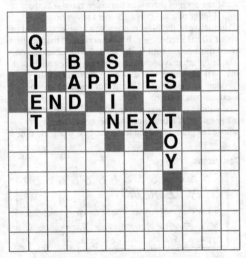

A time limit should be agreed; about 10 to 15 minutes should be sufficient.

Scoring

Each letter in a complete word is worth one point. The winner is the one with the highest score.

In the example on the previous page, the player has managed to use 22 of the letters in the time available. The score is 28: one point for each letter of each word.

TELEGRAMS

Players are given or make up a list of 15 letters and must use each of them – in the order given – as the initial letter of a word in a 15-word telegram. (Alternatively, the players are given or select a word of about 10 to 15 letters, e.g. **blackberries**, so that the first word must begin with B, the second with L, and so on.) The telegram may include one or two place names and may – if the player wishes – have the name of the 'sender' as the last word. Stops (or periods) may be used for punctuation.

The winner is the first player to complete their telegram, or, if a time limit has been set, the player whose telegram is judged to be the best when the time is up.

Telegrams

BLACKBERRIES

BRING LAMP AND CHISEL STOP KNOW
BEST ENTRY ROUTE STOP REST IS EASY
STOP SID

CONSEQUENCES 🛶 ✈ 🚤

This popular old game is interesting to play when there are three or more people.

Each player needs a strip of paper.

Playing

There are many versions of this game. In the original version, players begin by writing a boy's name on their pieces of paper, then folding them down so that nobody can see them. The papers are then passed to the person on the left of each player.

Everyone writes down a girl's name, folds it down and passes the paper on as before.

The game proceeds until each category, given in the first list below, has been completed.

Finally, the last players unravel the pieces of paper and read each story out loud.

Consequences: lists

traditional consequences

1 boy's name . . . met . . .
2 girl's name
3 where they met
4 he said
5 she said
6 what they did
7 and the consequences were . . .

the court case

1 the name of the accused . . . is accused of . . .
2 the charge
3 what the defence said
4 what the prosecution said
5 what the judge said
6 the verdict and outcome

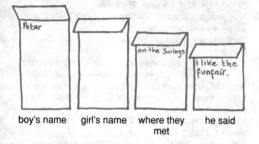

boy's name   girl's name   where they met   he said

the witch's potion
1 Into the cauldron was put . . .
2 and . . . next ingredient
3 next ingredient
4 last ingredient
5 what the witch did then
6 what the witch said
7 who drank the potion
8 the result

Creative ideas can be used to make other lists, such as 'space adventure', 'computer game' or 'news report'.

PICTURE CONSEQUENCES

This game has similarities with standard Consequences, but instead of writing words the players draw parts of an animal or a person, dressed in funny clothing, starting with the head and finishing with the feet. When the pieces of paper are folded over, part of the previous drawing is left showing, so as to give a lead to the next player. For example, after drawing the head,

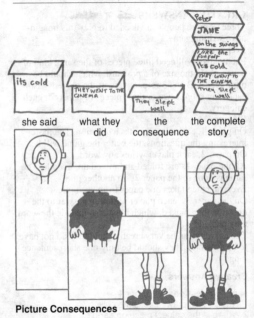

she said   what they   the   the complete
did   consequence   story

Picture Consequences

the paper should be folded so that the edges of the neck
are showing.

After drawing the feet, players may write down the
name of the person whom they want the figure to
represent!

CREATIVE ANSWERS 🚣 ✈ 🚢

Three or more people are needed to play this imaginative writing game.

Preparing

Each player will need three pieces of the same kind of paper, about the size of a postcard, which should be numbered 1, 2 and 3 respectively. If the players wish, each may submit two or three pieces of paper for each category.

Playing

On paper 1, each player writes a question. The more interesting the questions, the better the game will be.

On paper 2, each player writes any word.

All the paper 1s are folded and mixed up in a pile. The same is done to the paper 2s, in another pile.

Everyone then takes one paper from each pile.

On the paper 3s, each player writes an answer to the question they picked, which must also include the word they picked.

The answers can be very creative, and they do not have to be sensible! They should be only one short sentence long.

Creative Answers

sample questions on paper 1

1 Why do flies crawl across the ceiling?
2 Where is the coldest place on earth?
3 Who is the most important person here?
4 When will the end of the world come?
5 Why is the biro pen you select always dry ?
6 Why do coins always fall down the back of sofas ?
7 When do squirrels learn how to look for their nuts ?

sample words on paper 2

igloo	romantic	fur hat
Saturday	lorry	ducks
	moustache	

If a player were to select question 7, 'When do squirrels learn how to look for their nuts?' and the word **igloo**, they might write, 'Every year, when the thought of spring comes and igloos start to melt, mummy and daddy squirrels teach their baby squirrels to search for the winter store of nuts.' If they select the word **moustache**, the answer might be 'Each spring, when the squirrel's whiskers grow longer (it looks like some seem to have a moustache) it knows, when it drinks water, that it is time to look for its nuts.'

HANGMAN

Hangman is a popular game for two or more players. One person thinks of a word that has about five or six letters. They make the same number of dashes as there are letters in the chosen word.

The other players may then start guessing the letters in the word, calling out one letter at a time. If the guess is a successful one, the letter is written, by the first player, above the appropriate dash – if it appears more than once in the word, it must be entered as often as it occurs.

If the guess is an incorrect one, however, the first player may start to draw a hanged man. One line of the drawing represents each wrong letter; and the incorrect letter is written beneath the line of dashes so that the players can see what has been called.

If one of the other players guesses the word (this should

become easier as the game progresses) they may choose a word. If the hanged man is completed before the word is guessed, the first player may choose another word. To make the game more difficult, longer words can be chosen. Alternatively, the player could choose a group of words that forms a proverb or the title of a book or film – and the other players should be given a clue concerning the category.

A typical sequence is shown below and on the next two pages.

Hangman

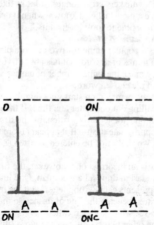

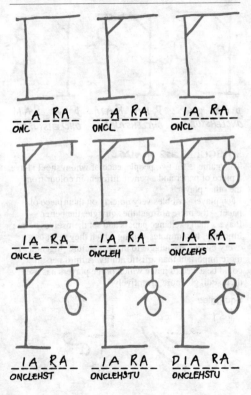

_ _ A _ _RA _
ONC

_ _ A _ _RA _
ONCL

_ I A _ _RA _
ONCL

_ I A _ _RA _
ONCLE

_ I A _ _RA _ _
ONCLEH

_ I A _ _RA _
ONCLEHS

_ I A _ _RA _ _
ONCLEHST

_ I A _ RA _
ONCLEHSTU

D I A _ RA _
ONCLEHSTU

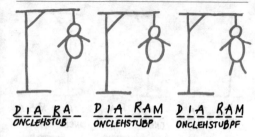

SQUIGGLES

This game is for two people, each of whom should have
a piece of paper and a pencil different in colour from
the other player's.

Each player scribbles very quickly on their piece of
paper – the more abstract the squiggle, the better.
Players then exchange papers and set themselves a time
limit, e.g. two minutes, during which they must use
every bit of the squiggle to make a picture. Ingenuity is
more important than artistic ability. A third person
could be asked to judge which of the players has used
their squiggle more inventively.

Squiggles

stage 1

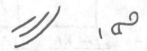

Squiggles

stage 2

NOUGHTS AND CROSSES

A favourite for generations, this game for two people is sometimes over in a matter of seconds!

Two vertical lines are drawn with two horizontal lines crossing them, forming nine spaces. Players decide which of them is to draw noughts (circles) and which of them crosses.

Taking turns alternately, the players make their mark in any vacant space until one of them manages to get three of his marks in a row (either horizontally, vertically or diagonally).

The winner draws a line through the winning row and the game comes to an end.

If neither player succeeds in forming a row, the game is considered drawn.

As the player who makes their mark first has a better chance of winning, players usually take it in turns to start each game.

Noughts and Crosses: sample play

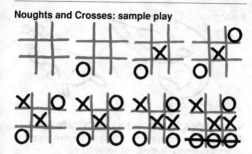

THREE-DIMENSIONAL NOUGHTS AND CROSSES

Based on the standard game, the three-dimensional version offers a lengthier and more challenging alternative. Three-dimensional Noughts and Crosses can be bought as a game, but can equally well be played with pencil and paper.

The game is played on a series of grids – each representing a different level. If there are four levels each of them is divided into four-by-four squares, making a playing area of 64 squares. Playing procedure is similar to standard Noughts and Crosses, but the winner is the first player to get four of his marks in a row on the same level or all four levels. Possible winning rows are shown on pp.180–181.

Three-dimensional Noughts and Crosses

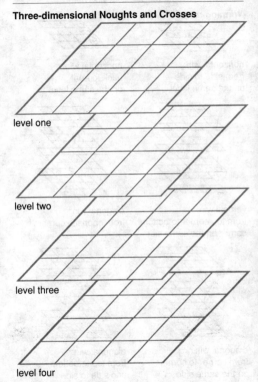

level one

level two

level three

level four

Winning rows

horizontal win:
from side to side
on the same level

horizontal win:
back to front
on the same level

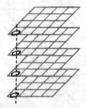

vertical win:
from top corner to bottom
corner on the same side

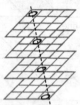

diagonal win:
from opposite corners

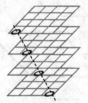

diagonal win:
from corner to corner
on the same side

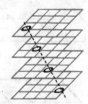

diagonal win:
from top to bottom
and side to side

	level one	level two	level three	level four

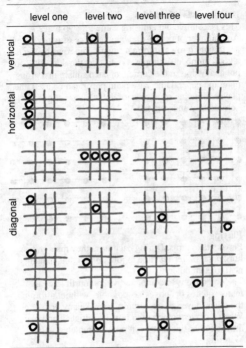

vertical

horizontal

diagonal

BOXES

This is a simple but amusing game for two players.
Any number of dots is drawn on a piece of paper. They
are drawn in rows to form a square. Ten rows by ten is
a good number. A simple way to map the dots out is to
put heavy dots at the corners of each square in a group
on graph paper. Otherwise plain paper can be used, the
players drawing even rows of dots that are aligned
horizontally and vertically.

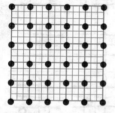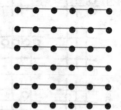

Playing

Players take turns. During each turn, they may draw a
horizontal or vertical line to join up two dots that are
next to each other.
The objective is to complete (with a fourth line) as
many squares or 'boxes' as possible, without affording
the other player an opportunity to make any boxes.
When a player completes a box, he initials it and may
draw another line that, preferably, completes a box.

Winning

When there are no more dots to be joined (as all the
boxes have been made) the game ends. The player with
the highest number of initialled boxes is the winner.

Variation

Another way of playing is to try to form the lowest possible number of boxes. The players join up as many dots as they can before being forced to complete a box. The winner is the player with the fewest initialled boxes.

Boxes: sample play

BATTLESHIPS

This is an extremely popular game for two players, each of whom needs a pencil and a sheet of squared (graph) paper.

The players should sit so that they cannot see each other's pieces of paper.

Both of them draw two identical grids, ten squares by ten in size.

In order to identify each square, the grids need numbers down one side and letters across the top (thus the top left-hand square is A1; the bottom right-hand square is J10, etc.).

Each player labels one grid as the 'home fleet' and the other grid as the 'enemy fleet'.

Both players have their own fleet of ships that they may position anywhere within the home-fleet grid.

A fleet is comprised of:

1 one battleship, four squares long;
2 two cruisers, each three squares long;
3 three destroyers, each two squares long;
4 four submarines, each taking up one square only.

Battleships: the fleet

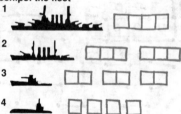

Ships are positioned by outlining the appropriate number of squares.

The squares representing each ship must be in a horizontal row or vertical column. There must also be at least one vacant square between the ships.

Playing

The objective is to destroy the opponent's entire fleet

Battleships: player 1's positions

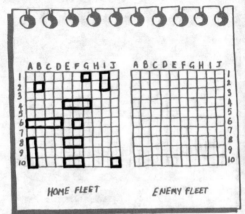

HOME FLEET   ENEMY FLEET

with a series of 'hits'. Players take turns.

During each turn, a player may attempt three hits, marking them on the enemy-fleet grid as they do so. The opponent must then consult their own home-fleet grid to see whether any of the squares are occupied. If they are, the opponent must state the number of squares and the category of ship hit.

In order to sink a ship, every one of its component squares must be hit. The game continues, with both players marking the state of their own and the enemy's fleet: this may be done by shading or outlining squares, or in some other manner.

Battleships: player 2's positions

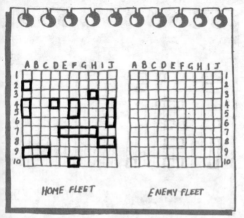

There is no limit to the number of hits each player may attempt. The game comes to an end as soon as one player entirely destroys their opponent's fleet.

BURIED TREASURE

This is a much simpler version of Battleships and it is particularly suitable for young children. It is a game for two, with a third person needed to help at the beginning of the game.

Each player draws a grid of nine squares by seven and labels the squares in the same way as for Battleships. The third person designates four of the nine letters from A to I to one player, and four of the remaining letters to the second player. One letter will be left over. Then allocate three numbers, from 1 to 7, to each player. One number will be left over.

Neither player knows which letters and numbers have been designated to their opponent. Also, they do not know which of the letters and numbers have not been allocated: these indicate the square with the 'buried treasure', and the players must try to identify it.

Buried Treasure: players' designated letters and numbers

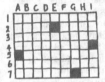

player 1

player 2

Player 1 received A5, E2, G7 and I4 as their squares. Player 2 received B3, D4, F5 and H6. The square in which the treasure is buried is C1.

Playing

The two players take it in turns to call out a letter and a number in the hope of locating, by a process of elimination, the buried treasure. Although they must always give truthful answers, players may call out a letter and number of a square that they hold themselves to bluff their opponent.

Winning

The first player to identify the square with the 'buried treasure' is the winner.

CRYSTALS 🚢 ✈ 🚚

In this game, players try to form 'crystal' patterns on
graph paper, using as many squares as possible.
Graph paper is required (at least half an A4 sheet for
every two players), and a different coloured pencil for
each player.

Playing

For the first round, each player selects a site for a
crystal area on the paper, by taking it in turns to shade
one square, using his or her coloured pencil. Each
shaded square represents one 'atom' of a final crystal.
For the following rounds, players may shade in other
single squares around the paper to claim various
crystal-building sites. Once they have done so, they will
begin to recognize which are the best-placed atoms for
crystal building. Players can begin to build on their own
single 'atoms' by shading in additional squares in
symmetrical patterns around the first squares. A
legitimate crystal may be formed from four or more
atoms drawn by one player only. A sample game is
shown on p. 190.

The rules for crystal building are as follows:

1 crystals must be symmetrical; (To determine this,
visualize lines drawn through four axes of the crystal:
vertical, horizontal and two diagonals. If the crystal can
be 'folded' along all of these axes, so that two halves
perfectly match one another, then the crystal is
symmetrical.)

2 crystals must contain at least four squares, all of
which have been shaded by one player only;

3 atoms must be connected at their sides, not at their
corners;

4 there must be no gaps or holes within the crystals.

Crystals: rules for building

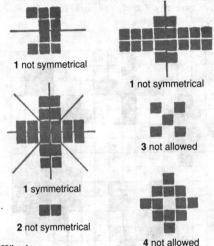

1 not symmetrical

1 not symmetrical

1 symmetrical

3 not allowed

2 not symmetrical

4 not allowed

Winning

As they complete crystals, players declare them as theirs and ring them, then move onto the next crystal. Players can try to block each other's building by forming crystals that use up the playing area (e.g. long and narrow crystals), or by blocking other players' crystal-building moves.

The game ends when no more crystals can be formed

because not enough empty squares remain on the paper. Players then count the number of squares each has filled in, making sure that the crystals conform to the rules of symmetry. The player with the highest number of shaded squares wins.

Crystals: example

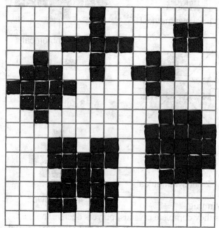

SPROUTS
A game, similar to boxes, requiring ingenuity to overcome seemingly simple problems.
It is a game for two players, each taking turns to add more lines to a design.

Sprouts: a sample game

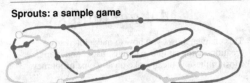

Playing

Six or more well-spaced dots are drawn (depending on the desired length of the game) on a sheet of paper. Taking turns, each player draws a line that joins two dots or which 'connects' a dot to itself. The player then adds another dot at any point to the line drawn, and their turn ends.

To provide a greater challenge, the following 'foul lines' are not permitted:

1 lines may not cross themselves;

2 lines may not cross other lines;

3 lines cannot be drawn through dots;

4 no dot may have more than three lines attached to it.

Winning

The last player able to draw a line, that conforms to the rules, is the winner.

Sprouts: foul lines

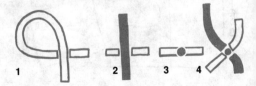

1   2   3   4

4. Making things

This chapter shows you how to make interesting creations using simple materials: paper and string. Most of these you can make on any type of journey.

Paper creations

Origami is the art of paper folding and is best carried out on a table surface – even a tray table on an aeroplane, train or coach will do. If travelling in a car, try using a large hardback book as a surface for folding. You might want to decorate your paper creations using crayons or coloured markers. If so, plan ahead – it is easier to decorate them before you have made them!

PAPER HAT ✘

1 You will need a piece of paper about 15 cm x 13 cm (6 in. x 5 in.).

2 Fold your piece of paper in half along the dotted line shown. (Be careful to fold along the width of the paper and not the length.) You should now have a rectangle.

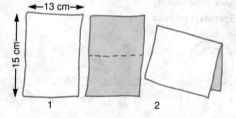

3 With the paper folded as in step **2**, fold over one of the corners as shown. Note that the corner which is folded in does not touch the bottom of your rectangle.

3

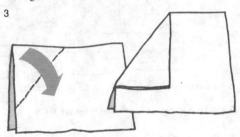

4 Fold over the other corner.

4

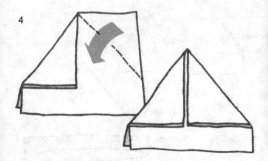

5 Fold up the bottom of the paper on one side.

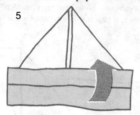

6 Turn the paper over and fold up the bottom on the other side.

7 Put your fingers inside the hat to open it up.

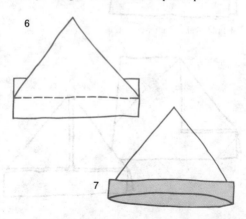

PAPER BOAT ✖

After making the Paper Hat, use your paper-folding
skills to create a boat.

1 Make the Paper Hat (see page 192).

2 Open the paper hat out as far as you can.

3 Squash the hat in half as shown. You should now
have a square-shaped piece of folded paper.

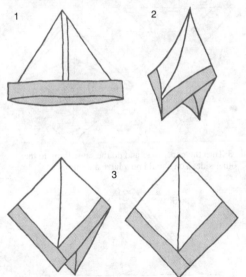

4 Along the dotted line shown, fold up one side of the new square which you have just created.

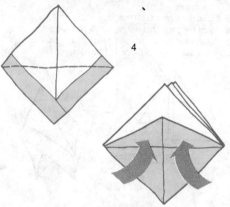

5 Turn the paper over and do the same thing to the other side. You should now have a triangle.

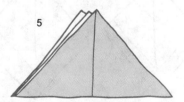

6 Put your fingers inside the triangle shape at the bottom (just like when you were opening out the hat) and open it out.

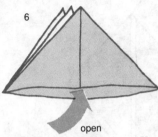

open

7 Squash your opened-out hat as shown. Your paper is now an even smaller square!

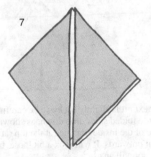

8 On one side, fold the bottom of the new, smaller square along the dotted line.

9 Turn the paper over and do the same thing on the other side. You should now have an even smaller triangle!

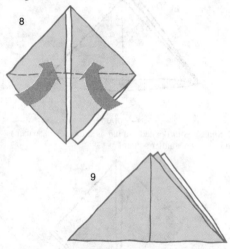

10 This next bit is slightly tricky so be careful! Let the two outside folded sides drop down, as shown. Then pinch one of the inside triangles at the top (at point **a**) and pull it outwards. It will look a bit loose, but the boat will not pull apart.

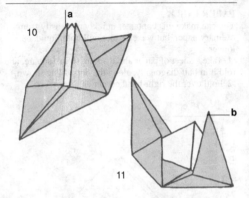

11 Now pull outwards on the opposite inside triangle (at point **b**).

12 Gently press the finished boat into shape.

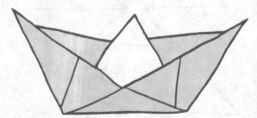

PAPER CUP ✖

You can make this container quickly and easily from
ordinary paper, but waxed paper will hold liquids
longer.

1 Take a sheet of paper about 15 cm (6 in.) square, and
fold it in half diagonally, along the dotted line shown.

2 Fold over the right-hand corner as shown.

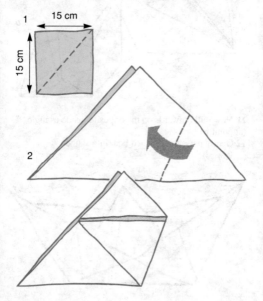

3 Tuck the nearest piece of the top triangle of paper into the right-hand piece that you have just folded over.

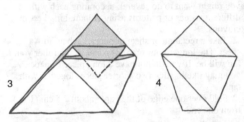

4 Turn the paper over and fold over the other corner of the triangle (the one that was the left corner) as shown.

5 Again, tuck the second top triangle into the pocket that you have just made.

6 Press gently against the outer edges and insert a finger into the centre space to open out the cup.

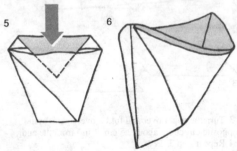

PAPER FAN ✖

This fan is easy and, with practice, quick to make – so you might want to do several, decorating each with different scenes or patterns using coloured markers or crayons.

1 Take a rectangular sheet of paper, such as an A4 sheet. The longer your piece of paper is, the fuller your fan will be. If you do not have a long piece of paper, you may like to stick two shorter pieces together with tape.

2 Fold over one edge of the paper about 2.5 cm (1 in.) from one end.

Note: The smaller each fold is, the more corrugated the fan will be when you have finished.

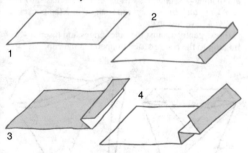

3 Turn the paper over and fold it over again, in the opposite direction, about 2.5 cm (1 in.) from the end.
4 Repeat step **3**.

5 Continue folding the paper over on alternate sides until you have made a kind of concertina or accordion of the entire sheet of paper.

5

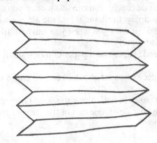

6 Grasp one side of the folded edges together to form a base. Fold over the base of the concertina two or three times, each time by about 1.25 cm (0.5 in.). This will help to hold the fan together. Alternatively, you could use a paper clip to hold the base of the fan together.

6

PAPER HELICOPTER ✖

This helicopter can be made anywhere, but cannot be tested while you are travelling in an enclosed space such as a car or coach. You can test it once you alight from your journey, throwing it into the air like a dart. Be sure to take it with you when you leave, or to dispose of it properly.

You will need: paper and a paper clip or a small hairpin.

1 Take a piece of paper about 20 cm x 5 cm (8 in. x 2 in.).

2 Fold the paper in half, along the dotted line shown.

3 Carefully tear down one end of the crease for about 5 cm (2 in.).

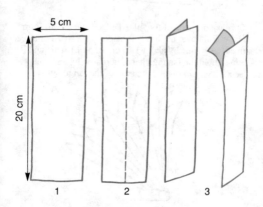

4 Fold down the two flaps that you have torn, using a firm crease. Let them stick out from the paper as shown.

5 Fold the base of the paper along the dotted lines. The paper should be folded over once on each side – do not fold both onto the same side.

6 Attach a paper clip or hairpin to the base of the paper helicopter as a weight.

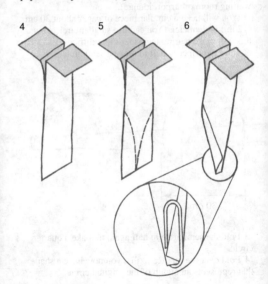

PAPER PICNIC TABLE MAT ✖

For this activity it is best to use very thin paper, such as pieces of newspaper or tissue paper. You might like to design your pattern first by lightly sketching the shapes that you want to tear out.

Paper tearing can make a mess (as loose pieces of torn paper are discarded) and you may want to take a small bag to collect these pieces in (especially if you are in a waiting room or airport lounge).

 1 You will need a circular piece of paper about 30 cm (12 in.) in diameter. (You can use smaller circles, but this will make tearing the paper more difficult.)

 2 Fold the paper in half to make a semicircle.

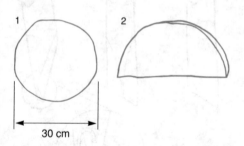

 3 Fold the semicircle in half again to make a quarter circle.

 4 Fold over the quarter so that you now have a shape that represents an eighth of the original circle.

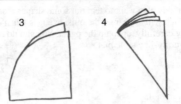

5 Now tear out shapes from either side of the folded piece you have made.

Note: If you have difficulty tearing the paper, open it out to a quarter circle (step **3**) and try again – it should now be easier to tear. Also, be careful not to tear right across from one side of the paper to the other – otherwise your table mat will be very small indeed!

6 You may also want to tear out some shapes along the top, which will appear on the outside edges when open.

7 Very carefully, open up the paper. You should now have a doily-like table mat.

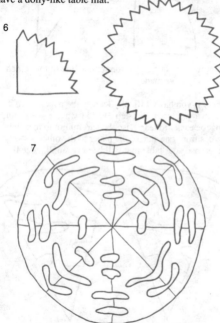

PAPER TREE ✖

Paper trees are best made from several sheets of thin paper, such as newspaper or tissue paper.

1 Take a large sheet of newspaper (the larger the better).

2 Roll up the newspaper to form a tube. Note: Roll from the shortest side and not the longest.

3 The diameter of your tube should measure about 1.25 cm (0.5 in.).

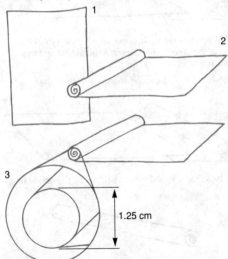

4 When you are about 10 cm (4 in.) from the end of the sheet of newspaper, insert another sheet as shown. Continue rolling with this second sheet in place.

first sheet   second sheet

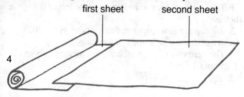

5 When you are again about 10 cm (4 in.) from the end of the second sheet, insert a third sheet and this time roll it all the way up.

first and second sheet   third sheet

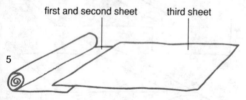

6 Bend the finished tube in half, along the dotted line.

7 Unbend the tube and flatten one of the halves. Tear down along the centre of the flattened half.

8 Now tear the already torn strips in half.

You should now have a tube that is torn into four strips at one end.

9 Holding the bottom half of the tube (the round part, not the torn, flattened part), grasp the innermost torn pieces with your other hand and gently pull them out to form a 'tree'. Be careful not to tear the 'leaves' as you pull them.

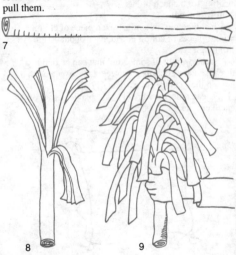

String and wool creations

Some of these activities involve cutting. Use plastic,
round-ended scissors only. If travelling in a car or other
jolting vehicle, have an adult use the scissors to do any
cutting necessary.

PARACHUTE ✖

This parachute can be made while travelling by car but
should only be tested in the open where you have more
space, such as at an airport or train station, or while
waiting for a coach or bus.

You will need:

● A handkerchief or similar-sized piece of cloth.
● Four pieces of cotton thread, each about 40 cm (16
in.) long.
● A small weight of some kind that can be tied to a
thread, such as buttons or sweets (any sweets with a
hole in their centre are particularly good).

 1 Tie each piece of thread to a separate corner of the
handkerchief.

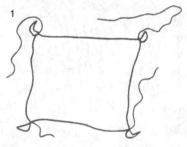

2 Knot all four pieces of thread together near to their other ends, leaving some of the ends to trail loosely.

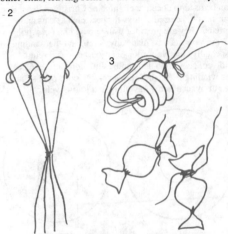

3 Tie your small weight(s) to the base of the parachute. Objects with a hole in the centre can be threaded onto the loose ends, which are then looped around and knotted as shown. Other small objects can be tied to the end of each thread on the parachute.

You may need to experiment a bit with different weights to find the type you prefer. For this reason it is best not to tie your weight too securely – in case you need to untie it again and replace it with another!

WOOL BALLS ✖

These wool balls – 'pom-poms' – are easy to make and can be used to decorate clothing or Christmas trees, or can simply be used as toys for pets such as cats and kittens. They are great for using up odd bits of wool.

Pom-poms can be made anywhere, and the winding is especially suitable for long car journeys as it requires little concentration and can be time-consuming. Once the winding is finished, however, the pom-pom should be cut by an adult if travelling in a jolting vehicle.

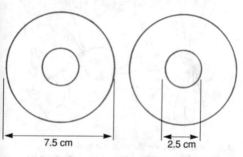

7.5 cm   2.5 cm

You will need:
- Two discs or rings of card, each measuring about 7.5 cm (3 in.) in diameter. The hole in the centre of the discs should be at least 2.5 cm (1 in.) in diameter. Pom-poms can be made with varying sizes of card template – smaller ones use less wool and are quicker to make but can be more difficult to handle; larger ones take a long time to make and require more wool.

● A small ball of wool. It needs to be small enough to push through the centre hole in the discs. Use a medium thickness yarn if you have never made pom-poms before. Thick wools create lovely pom-poms quickly, but can be difficult to cut through. Thin wools take a long time to wind. You can also mix the colours of the wool by winding, for example, three strands of yarn at once instead of one.

● A 20-cm length of yarn to tie the centre of the pom-pom together.

● A pair of round-ended scissors.

1 Place the two circles of card together so that the centre holes are aligned.

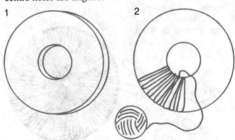

2 Wind the wool around the rings as shown. Eventually, the ball of wool may not fit through the centre hole and you might need to unravel it a little or squash it to make it fit. With practice you will quickly learn which is the best wool to use, how much you need and how long it will take you.

3 Wind the wool around the rings until they are completely covered or until you have run out of wool. If you are ready to stop winding but have not run out of wool, simply cut the wool to about the edge of the discs.

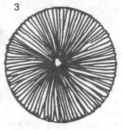

4 Using your scissors, cut between the card discs, cutting through the wool.

5 You will now have a wool ball with two card discs in its centre. Take a piece of yarn (long enough to hang up the ball if necessary) and wind it TIGHTLY around the centre of the ball, in between the two pieces of card. If you do not tie the wool tightly the pom-pom may fall apart. Knot the two ends of this piece of yarn securely.

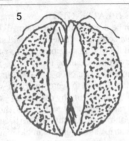

6 Remove the card by carefully cutting to the centre of each disc and pulling it away and out of the pom-pom.

7 Fluff out the finished pom-pom with your fingers.

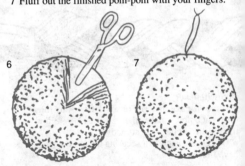

You can use the yarn coming from the centre of the pom-pom to hang it or attach it to a piece of clothing. Alternatively, trim the yarn close to the edge of the ball.

BRAIDING (PLAITING) ✂

Braiding can be done almost anywhere. You can braid
long hair on a companion's head or braid strips of
fabric or lengths of thin rope or wool. Even strips of
strong paper or plastic can be used.

Whichever material you choose to braid (except hair, of
course!), you will need to secure one end while you
work. If you are travelling by car and the seat in front
of you has a raised headrest, you can tie the strips or
pieces of wool to that. Another way to secure the braid
is to tape the strips at one end to an old magazine or
other flat surface. Alternatively, have a friend sit
opposite you to hold one end while you braid.

A finished braid

You will need:

● Three strips of material or wool. Choosing three
different colours makes the steps easier to follow and
the finished braid more attractive.
● Two elastic bands for securing the braid once you
have finished.

The illustrations show strips of fabric being braided,
but the procedure would be the same whatever the
material used.

1 Secure the ends of the strips of material or pieces of wool.

2 Take the strip on the far right and bring it to the centre, positioning it between the other two strips.

3 Take the far left strip and bring it to the centre, positioning it between the other two strips.

4 Repeat steps **2** and **3**, alternating the left-hand strip and right-hand strip, until you have used up all of your braiding material.

5 Secure your braid at the bottom with the elastic band. Carefully detach the top ends that were secured and tie them with the second elastic band.

If you experiment, you will quickly learn which is the best way to hold the braid while you are working on it.

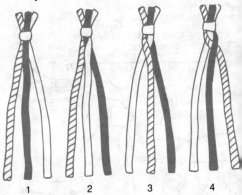

1   2   3   4

KNITTING ON A BOBBIN ✖

This activity is very simple, yet it allows children to
create a length of knitted cord in a relatively short
time. It can be carried out safely in any moving vehicle.

You will need:

● An old wooden thread bobbin with four small nails
fixed to one end, as shown. This must be assembled
before the journey. (If a wooden bobbin cannot be
found, a cork can be used: make a large hole in the
centre, all the way through, and push four pins or nails
around the edge of the hole.)
● A ball of wool or string. The thinner the wool or
string, the thinner the final knitted cord will be. Avoid
large and fluffy wool like mohair, and instead use wool
or string of a medium thickness.
● A crochet hook, cocktail stick or sharpened pencil.

1 Tie your string or wool to one of the small nails.
2 Loop the string around each nail as shown.

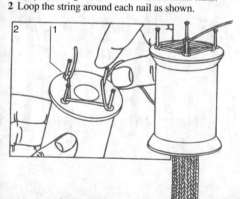

3 When you have looped all the nails once around,
start to wind the string around the nails for the second
time. Instead of looping the complete nail, however, use
your cocktail stick or crochet hook to lift up the
previous loop and hook it over the nail and over the
string you are working with, as shown.

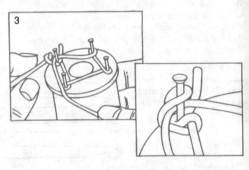

Continue in this way, working round and round the
bobbin. At the beginning, push the cord that is forming
down through the hole in the bobbin. As you knit, the
cord will work its way through the hole on its own, and
will eventually emerge from the hole at the bottom of
the bobbin. The thicker your wool or string, the quicker
this cord will emerge.

When you have run out of string, or when the cord is as
long as you want it, secure the string by winding it one
last time around, passing it up through each outside
loop as you go.

CROCHET ✖

Crochet is a method of knotting a thread by drawing it into a chain by means of a hook. Beautiful patterns can be made by varying the number and combination of knots, and it is an activity which can be carried out in a confined space on any type of journey.

Be careful when using the crochet hook in a moving vehicle, and never point it at anyone.

Illustrated here are the basic crochet stitches; using these, you can crochet a simple, rectangular piece of work even while travelling.

You will need:

● A crochet hook. These come in a variety of sizes. A largish hook is best for children.

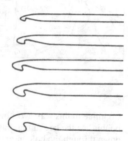

● A ball of soft string or wool. Crochet can be used to make anything from delicate lace to chunky macrame. For this reason it is best to choose a very thin, lightweight thread for use with a small crochet hook, and larger, heavier cords and wools for use with bigger crochet hooks. It is best to avoid fluffy wools – such as mohair and angora – as these may make it difficult for children to follow the step-by-step instructions.

Basic chain stitch

This is a long line of stitches onto which all other stitches are attached. It forms the base of your crochet work.

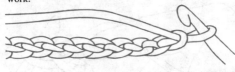

1 Make a slipknot around the crochet hook and pull both ends of the yarn to tighten it.

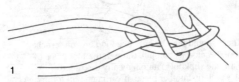

1

2 Holding the base of the slipknot in your left hand, hook a piece of yarn with the crochet hook.

2

3 Pull it back through the loop that is already on your hook.

3

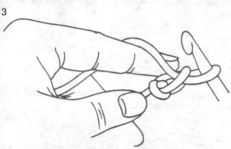

There should now be only one loop on your crochet hook because as you pull through the first piece of yarn, the slipknot is automatically discarded.

4 Catch up another piece of yarn and pull it through the existing loop on your crochet hook. Again, you should be left with only one loop on your hook – the new one that you have just made.

5 Continue in this way until you have a 'chain' about 10 cm (4 in.) long.

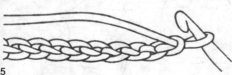

5

Basic crochet stitch

The next set of steps shows you how to build on the chain stitch to make connected rows of crochet work. Beginners may find that it takes them some time to master this technique because it can be quite tedious, but with a little practice crocheting can be quick and neat.

6 Take the length of chain you made in the previous steps. Place your hook back through the chain at the second hole, as shown.

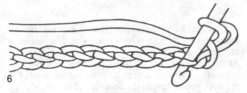

6

7 Once you have pushed your hook through the chain stitch, hook a piece of yarn.

Note: As you work, you will turn the chain over to see where the hook comes out at the other side. This 'bottom' view is shown here.

7

8 Pull this new piece of yarn back through the chain stitch. You now have two stitches on your hook.

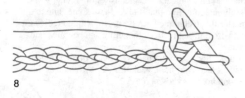

9 Catch up the yarn again and draw it through both loops on your hook. You have made your first single crochet stitch!
At the beginning, your chain will probably not look impressive – it takes time to build up and the more of the work you complete, the better it looks.

10 Repeat steps **6** to **9** until you have finished your line of stitches. At the end of the row make a single chain stitch and turn the work round.

11 Begin a new row by inserting your hook into the first stitch.

11

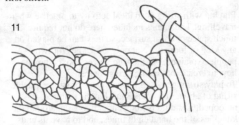

Continue in this way until you have built up rows of crochet.

12 Finish your crochet work by simply pulling the yarn through the last stitch on your hook, as shown.

12

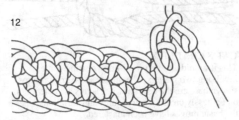

5. String games

Playing with string is an ideal activity to practise when travelling. The games included here do not require much space or a flat surface, so they can be played on any kind of journey. Not only are games for two people explained, but the solo player, too, is shown how to create interesting string figures.

To play string games, a looped piece of strong, pliable string of about 185 cm (73 in.) long is required. If unlooped, it should be long enough to wrap around the knuckles of the hand eight times, and to have its ends joined together with a square or reef knot, thus making a loop.

A reef knot

CAT'S CRADLE ✖

This is an old and very well-known string game, involving two players. The moves and named figures shown here are the best known. Players are able to go on endlessly creating new figures and variations, once the basic moves have been mastered.

1 Player 1 loops the string once around each wrist, keeping the two lines of string parallel.

2 The right forefinger is pushed under the line in front of the left wrist.

3 The left forefinger is then pushed under the line in front of the right wrist.
4 The string is pulled tight to reveal the 'cat's cradle'.

Cat's Cradle

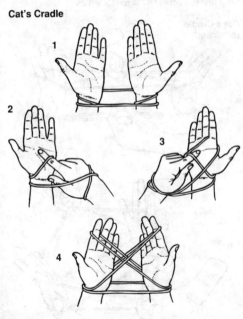

cat's cradle

5 Player 2 takes hold of the lines that cross over, between Player 1's hands, from the side.
6 The lines are pulled out, down and under the parallel lines that run between Player 1's wrists.

Cat's Cradle
(continued)

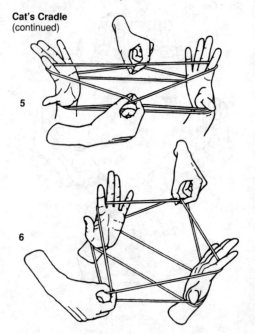

7 Player 2 pushes the lines up, inside the parallel lines.
8 Player 1 lets go and Player 2 stretches the thumbs and forefingers apart to reveal the 'mattress'.

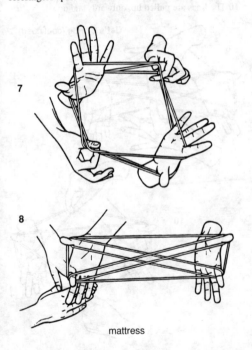

mattress

9 Player 1 takes hold of the string from above, at the point where the long lines cross over, with the thumbs and forefingers.

10 The lines are pulled up, outwards and down.

Cat's Cradle (continued)

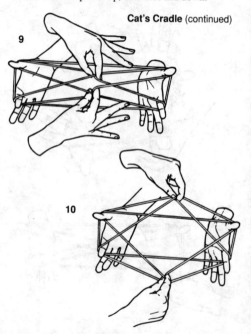

11 They are then pushed up inside the long, parallel lines.

12 Player 2 lets go of the string, while Player 1 pulls the hands apart, straightening and stretching the thumbs and forefingers to reveal the 'calm sea' (or 'tramlines').

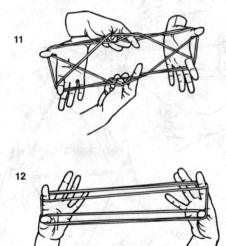

calm sea

13 Player 2 pulls the single line on the left to the right with the right little finger.
14 The single line on the right is pulled to the left with the left little finger.

Cat's Cradle (continued)

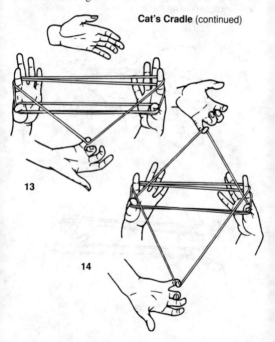

13

14

15 Player 2 brings the hands down (while turning them over so that the thumbs and forefingers point inwards), and then brings them up inside the double lines, taking the lines onto the outstretched thumbs and forefingers.
16 Player 1 lets go of the string and Player 2 spreads the thumbs and forefingers to reveal the 'upturned cradle'.

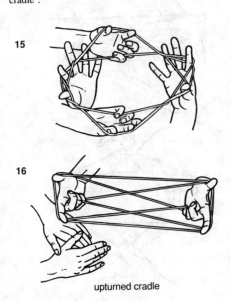

15

16

upturned cradle

17 Player 1 takes hold of the lines that cross over, from the side, with the forefingers and thumbs.

18 Player 1 pulls the crossed lines out and up, over and down inside the long, parallel lines.

Cat's Cradle (continued)

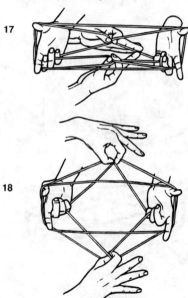

17

18

19 As Player 1's hands move down, inside the parallel lines, the forefingers and thumbs are stretched out, and the hands are moved apart, so that the string is taken from Player 2.

20 Player 2 lets go of the string and Player 1 spreads the thumbs and forefingers further to reveal the 'mattress turned over'.

19

20

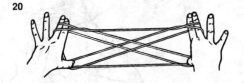

mattress turned over

21 Player 2 takes the crossed long lines from above and pulls them up, sideways and down.

22 Player 2 then pushes up from underneath, on the inside of the long, parallel lines, with the thumbs and forefingers stretched out, taking up the long, parallel lines.

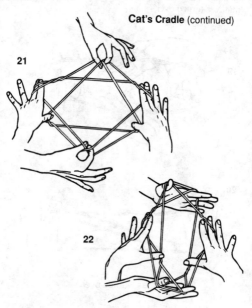

Cat's Cradle (continued)

21

22

23 Player 1 lets go. Player 2 spreads the thumbs and
forefingers to reveal the 'cat's eye'.
24 Player 1 takes hold of the string, at the points where
the diagonal and parallel lines cross over, and pulls
them outwards.

23

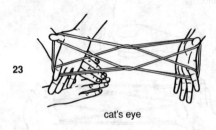

cat's eye

24

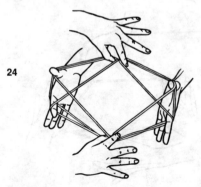

25 Player 2 lets go.
26 Player 2 takes hold of the lines that cross over, from above.

Cat's Cradle
(continued)

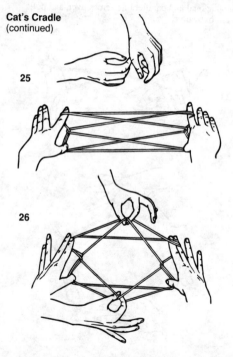

25

26

27 The lines are taken under the long, parallel lines, which are taken on to Player 2's straightened thumbs and forefingers.

28 Player 1 lets go.

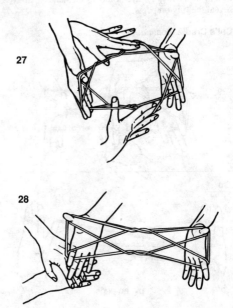

29 Player 1 takes hold of the string, at the point where the long, parallel lines intersect with the diagonal lines, from above, and turns the forefingers and thumbs in and up, and pulls the string out.

30 Player 2 lets go. Player 1 moves the hands apart to reveal the 'pig on pegs'.

Cat's Cradle (continued)

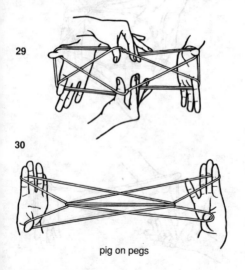

29

30

pig on pegs

String figures

These string games are for solo players.
THE RIBCAGE ✖
1 Place the string behind both little fingers, across the palms and behind the thumbs.
2 Put the lines that are across each palm behind the middle finger of each hand.

The Ribcage

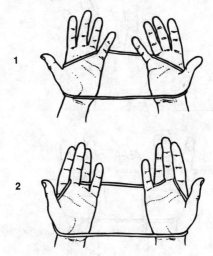

3 Push the right forefinger, from below, under the front forefinger line of the left hand. Then push the right ring finger, from below, under the line in front of the ring finger of the left hand.

4 Pull the string tight.

The Ribcage (continued)

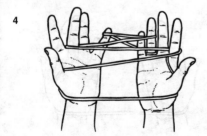

5 The forefinger and ring finger of the left hand then repeat the moves. Care must be taken to stay inside the lines.

6 Pull the string tight again, revealing the 'ribcage'.

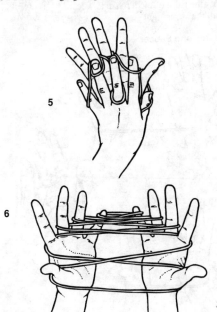

5

6

THE CUP AND SAUCER ✖

1 To begin, place the string behind both little fingers, across the palms and behind the thumbs.
2 Push the right forefinger under the line which runs across the palm of the left hand.
3 Pull the string tight.

The Cup and Saucer

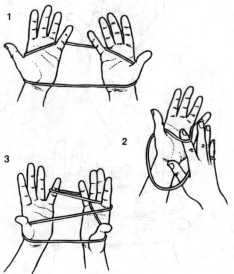

4 Push the left forefinger under the line which runs
across the palm of the right hand.
5 Pull the string tight.
6 Bend the thumbs over the crossed lines and under the
lines behind the forefingers.

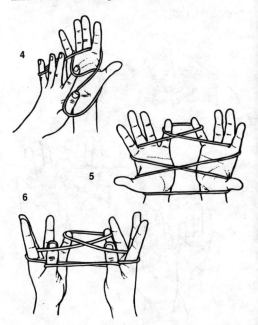

7 Then bend the thumbs round and down to pull the
lines behind the forefingers through the front line, so
that the front line slips off the thumbs.
8 Bend both little fingers forward.
9 Let the string fall off the little fingers.

The Cup and Saucer (continued)

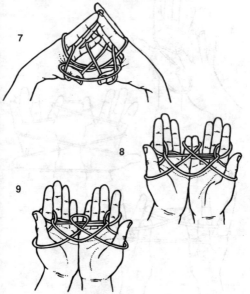

10 Move the hands apart, pulling the string tight.
11 Finally, turn the hands to reveal the 'cup and saucer'.

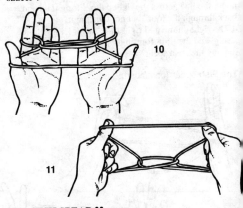

THE FISH SPEAR ✖

1 To begin, place the string behind both little fingers, across the palms and behind the thumbs.

The Fish Spear

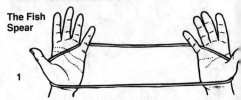

2 Push the right forefinger under the line across the left palm, pulling and twisting it twice, to form a loop.
3 Push the left forefinger through this loop and then under the line across the right palm, lifting it up and back through the loop, but not twisting it.
4 The right thumb and right little finger let go of the string, and the right forefinger pulls the string tight, making the 'fish spear'.

The Fish spear (continued)

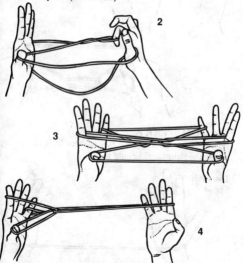

THE FLY ✖

Also known as the 'mosquito' and 'smashing the coconut', this game has a surprise ending.

1 Place the string over both thumbs.

2 The right hand lifts both lines over and behind the left hand.

3 Pull the string tight.

The Fly

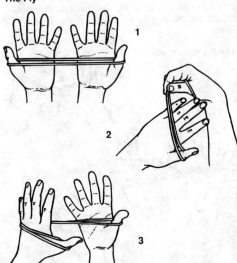

4 From above, hook the little finger of the right hand round the double line at the back of the hand.

5 The right little finger then continues to pull the double line between the forefinger and thumb of the left hand.

6 The left little finger slides down the right palm, picking up the double line that is hooked on the right thumb.

7 The left little finger continues to pull the double line over the other four lines. The right hand then lifts the double line crossing the left forefinger over the left thumb.

The Fly (continued)

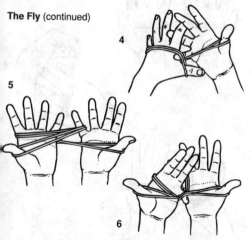

8 The right hand is used again to lift the double line from behind the left hand, over the left hand, allowing the lines to drop.

9 Stretch the hands and pull the string tight to reveal the 'fly'.

The final surprise comes when the hands are sharply clapped together, as if to kill the fly, while the loops are dropped off both little fingers. When the string is pulled tight again, the fly disappears and only a loop of string remains between the thumbs, which is how the game started.

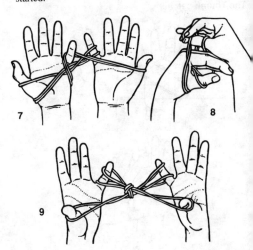

THE THUMB-CATCHER ✖

Most string games make patterns, but some perform
tricks. This is one of the latter kind.

1 To begin, place the string so that it is crossed between
the hands, with two lines going behind both little
fingers, across the palms and behind the thumbs.
The line going from in front of the left thumb to the
back of the right little finger should be on top.

2 Push the right forefinger under the line crossing the
left palm.

The Thumb-catcher

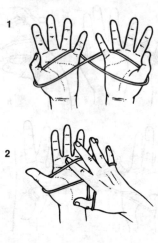

3 Push the left forefinger under the line crossing the right palm.
4 Pull the string tight.
5 Bend both thumbs down over the lines in front of the forefingers.

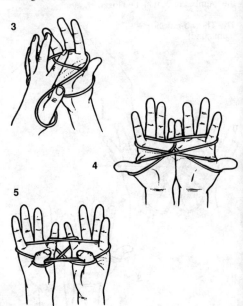

6 Push both thumbs down behind the lines, through and up again.

7 Remove both forefingers and little fingers from the string.

8 As the hands are opened and the string is pulled tight, the thumbs are caught, tied together.

The Thumb-catcher
(continued)

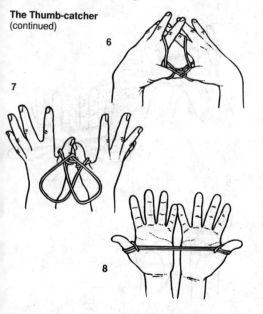